Exercises

to accompany

The Brief Penguin Handbook

Second Edition

by

Lester Faigley

University of Texas at Austin

PEARSON
Longman

New York Boston San Francisco
London Toronto Sydney Tokyo Singapore Madrid
Mexico City Munich Paris Cape Town Hong Kong Montreal

Exercises to accompany *The Brief Penguin Handbook, Second Edition*

ISBN: 0-321-33404-3

1 2 3 4 5 6 7 8 9 10–OPM–07 06 05

CONTENTS

Chapter 1, *The Rhetorical Situation* 1

Chapter 2, *Words, Images and Graphics* 5

Chapter 3, *Planning and Drafting* 7

Chapter 4, *Composing Paragraphs* 12

Chapter 5, *Rewriting, Editing, and Proofreading* 17

Chapter 6, *Critical Reading and Viewing* 21

Chapter 7, *Analyzing Verbal and Visual Texts* 22

Chapter 8, *Writing to Reflect* 23

Chapter 9, *Writing to Inform* 25

Chapter 10, *Writing to Persuade* 28

Chapter 11, *Design Basics* 31

Chapter 12, *Illustrations, Tables, and Charts* 32

Chapter 13, *Verbal and Visual Presentations* 34

Chapter 14, *Writing for the Web* 35

Chapter 15, *Planning Your Research* 36

Chapter 16, *Finding Print Sources in Libraries* 38

Chapter 17, *Finding Sources Online* 40

Chapter 18, *Evaluating Sources* 42

Chapter 19, *Avoiding Plagiarism When Using Sources* 44

Chapter 20, *Writing the Research Project* 49

Chapter 21, *MLA Documentation* 52

Chapter 22, *Writing About Literature* 54

Chapter 23, *APA Documentation* 56

Chapter 24, *CMS Documentation* 57

Chapter 25, *CSE Documentation* 58

Chapter 26, *Write with Power* 59

Chapter 27, *Write Concisely* 62

Chapter 28, *Write with Emphasis* 66

Chapter 29, *Find the Right Words* 69

Chapter 30, *Write to be Inclusive* 76

Chapter 31, *Write for Diverse Audiences* 79

Chapter 32, *Grammar Basics* 80

Chapter 33, *Fragments, Run-ons, and Comma Splices* 92

Chapter 34, *Subject-Verb Agreement* 96

Chapter 35, *Verbs* 101

Chapter 36, *Pronouns* 105

Chapter 37, *Modifiers* 110

Chapter 38, *Commas* 116

Chapter 39, *Semi-colons and Colons* 121

Chapter 40, *Hyphens* 123

Chapter 41, *Dashes and Parentheses* 124

Chapter 42, *Apostrophes* 126

Chapter 43, *Quotation Marks* 128

Chapter 44, *Other Punctuation Marks* 131

Chapter 45, *Write with Accurate Spelling* 135

Chapter 46, *Capitalization and Italics* 140

Chapter 47, *Abbreviations, Acronyms, and Numbers* 142

Chapter 48, *Writing in a Second Language* 145

Chapter 49, *Nouns and Articles* 146

Chapter 50, *Verbs* 150

Chapter 51, *English Sentence Structure* 154

Chapter 52, *Idiomatic Structures* 158

Sample Answers

EXERCISE 1-1 *Persuasive Appeals*

Read the following passages and decide which appeal (to logic, to credibility, to emotion) is being addressed.

1. "I wanted the perfect meal.
    I also wanted—to be absolutely frank—Col. Walter E. Kurtz, Lord Jim, Lawrence of Arabia, Kim Philby, the Consul, Fowler, Tony Po, B. Traven, Christopher Walken ... I wanted to find—no, wanted to be—one of those debauched heroes and villains out of Graham Greene, Joseph Conrad, Francis Coppola, and Micheal Cimino. I wanted to wander the world in a dirty seersucker suit, getting into trouble."

    —Anthony Bourdain, *A Cook's Tour,* 2001

Appeals to: _____

2. "Whenever any group can vote in a bloc, and decide the outcome of elections, and it *fails* to do this, then that group is politically sick. Immigrants once made Tammany Hall the most powerful single force in American politics. In 1880, New York City's first Irish Catholic was elected and by 1960 America had its first Irish Catholic President. America's black man, voting as a bloc, could wield an even more powerful bloc."

    —Malcolm X, *The Autobiography of Malcolm X*, 1965

Appeals to: _____

3.   "In times of crisis, we must all decide again and again whom we love."

> —Frank O'Hara, "To the Film Industry in Crisis," *Meditations in an Emergency*, 1957

Appeals to: _____

4.   "When in the course of human events, it becomes necessary for one people to dissolve the political bands which have connected them with one another, and to assume among the powers of the earth, the separate and equal station which the Laws of Nature and of Nature's God entitle them, a decent respect to the opinions of mankind requires that they should declare the causes which impel them to the separation."

> —Thomas Jefferson, *The Declaration of Independence*, 1776.

Appeals to: _____

5.   "I do not deeply distrust my country. She is not dead, but in my time she sleepeth, and the spirit of our fathers flames no more, but lies hid beneath the ashes."

> —Margaret Fuller, *Writings*, 1941.

Appeals to: _____

EXERCISE 1-2 *A Writer's Audience*

Suppose you are a freelance writer who has lined up several assignments for a variety of publications. Your topics and the publications are listed. Analyze your intended audience: how much information will they most likely have about your subject (much, none, some), what is their attitude likely to be (positive, negative, neutral), what will their interest level most likely be (low, moderate, high). In a few cases, you might need to do some research into the readership for the publication.

1.   a chapter about the Vietnam War for a high school textbook

---

2.   an article evaluating health care plans for *Modern Maturity*

---

3.   a profile of a prominent Republican senator for *Mother Jones*

---

4.   a feature on women's rights in the Middle East for Oprah Winfrey's magazine, *O*

---

5.   an article about the importance of emissions-control features for engines in *Car and Driver*

EXERCISE 1-3 *A Writer's Ethos*

Evaluate the following passages, as well as the example(s) of appeals to ethos you found in Exercise 1.1, for their appeals to credibility. What sort of ethos does the author present? How might this affect his or her presentation of the topic?

1. Topic: Colonialism
In Moulmein, in Lower Burma, I was hated by large numbers of people—the only time in my life that I have been important enough for this to happen to me. I was sub-divisional police officer of the town, and in an aimless, petty kind of way anti-European feeling was very bitter.
                                    —George Orwell, "Shooting an Elephant," 1936
2. Topic:
Yonder sky that has wept tears of compassion upon my people for centuries untold, and which to us appears changeless and eternal, may change. Today is fair. Tomorrow it may be overcast with clouds. My words are like the stars that never change. Whatever Seattle says, the great chief at Washington can rely upon with as much certainty as he can upon the return of the sun or the seasons. The white chief says that Big Chief at Washington sends us greetings of friendship and goodwill. This is kind of him for we know he has little need of our friendship in return. His people are many. They are like the grass that covers vast prairies. My people are few. They resemble the scattering trees of a storm-swept plain. The great, and I presume good, White Chief sends us word that he

wishes to buy land but is willing to allow us enough to live comfortably. This indeed appears just, even generous, for the Red Man no longer has rights that he need respect, and the offer may be wise, also, as we are no longer in need of an extensive country.

—Seattle, Chief of the Suquamish, Treaty Oration, 1854: originally published in the *Seattle Sunday Star*, 29 Oct. 1887.

3. Topic: The impeachment of President Nixon

We will not have Richard Nixon to kick around much longer—which is not especially "sorrowful news" to a lot of people, except that the purging of the cheap little bastard is going to have to take place here in Washington and will take up the rest of our summer.

—Hunter S. Thompson, "The Scum Also Rises," 1974

EXERCISE 2-1 *Images*

Think about the "dingbats" (the icons and symbols) that come with the font sets in a computer. Look at the following symbols and write out what each one is typically used to represent. Are there any that you don't know? Compare your answers with your classmates' answers. Do the meanings seem universal, or are meanings dependent on cultural factors?

1. _____
2. _____
3. _____
4. _____
5. _____
6. _____
7. _____
8. _____
9. _____
10. _____

EXERCISE 2-2 *Words or Visuals?*

Which of the following would be best represented by a visual? Which would be best represented by text? Which would benefit from both kinds of representation?

1. the definition of plagiarism *(visual/text/both)*
2. the increase in cases of plagiarism on college campuses each year since the Internet became readily available to students *(visual/text/both)*
3. other possible causes for the rise in plagiarism cases *(visual/text/both)*
4. a proposal for an advertising campaign alerting students to the possible penalties of plagiarism *(visual/text/both)*
5. instructions for kindergarten-age children for making a peanut butter and jelly sandwich *(visual/text/both)*
6. a complaint to your city's tenant council about the maintenance of your apartment complex *(visual/text/both)*
7. an agreement with your landlord dividing up responsibilities *(visual/text/both)*
8. an evaluation of NASCAR drivers *(visual/text/both)*
9. a comparison of the fighting styles of two martial arts masters *(visual/text/both)*
10. a description of renovations that should be made to the student gymnasium *(visual/text/both)*

EXERCISE 2-3 *For Practice: Words and Visuals*

Find an example of words and visuals used effectively to convey a message. This can be an advertisement, a poster announcing a public service, a brochure, an article in a periodical, a page in a textbook or book, a manual, a work of art, a flyer for a concert or show, a Web site, or anything else that appeals to you to use. Describe the work accomplished by the visuals and the text both separately and in combination with one another. Why is the example you've chosen effective?

Chapter 3
Planning and Drafting

EXERCISE 3-1 *Planning*

Make a list of topics you care about. Add to your list by taking a survey of topics your friends, classmates, and family members care about. Hold on to this list for future exercises.

EXERCISE 3-2 *Finding a Topic*

A student generated the following list for his research paper on the history of the horror movie. Choose a topic for the paper from the list. Then, organize his list into categories that the student could deal with in a paper. Eliminate any dead-end topics or redundancies.

Nosferatu (1922)
Bela Lugosi *Dracula* (1931)
Boris Karloff *Frankenstein* (1931)
Christopher Lee as Dracula in '60s
 monster movies
Creature from the Black Lagoon (1956)
werewolves
slasher films
women
Wes Craven *Scream* (1996)
Hammer Films and Christopher Lee
blood vs. suspense
Stephen King
mutants, aliens, robots 50s?
irony and independent film
demons/possession
what was scary then/now? ('20s-late '90s and beyond)
special effects
cult movies
Friday the 13th (1980)
cannibalism
Jamie Lee Curtis
The Exorcist (1973)
Carrie (1976)
weird trilogies they made in the '60s

Vincent Price as Dr. Phibes in '70s
teenagers in the woods
The Blair Witch Project (1999)
silent movies with haunted castles
Edgar Allen Poe popular in '70s

EXERCISE 3-3 *Exploring the Topic*

Read the passage below and freewrite for ten minutes. When you are done, look over what you wrote and pick out two or three topics that would be worth pursuing in a paper.

That in the beginning when the world was young there were a great many thoughts but no such thing as a truth. Man made the truths himself and each truth was a composite of a great many vague thoughts. All about in the world were the truths and they were all beautiful.

The old man had listed hundreds of the truths in his book. I will not try to tell you of all of them. There was the truth of virginity and the truth of passion, the truth of wealth and of poverty, of thrift and of profligacy, of carelessness and abandon. Hundreds and hundreds were the truths and they were all beautiful.

And then the people came along. Each as he appeared snatched up one of the truths and some who were quite strong snatched up a dozen of them.

It was the truths that made the people grotesques. The old man had quite an elaborate theory concerning the matter. It was his notion that the moment one of the people took one of the truths to himself, called it his truth, and tried to live his life by it, he became a grotesque and the truth he embraced became a falsehood.

—Sherwood Anderson, "The Book of the Grotesque," *Winesburg, Ohio*, 1919

Possible Topics:
_____
_____
_____
_____
_____

Exercise 3-4 *Reflective, Informative, Persuasive*

Look at the theses below. What kind (reflective, informative, persuasive) is each?

1. Reading Sylvia Plath's poem "Daddy" awakened me to the depth of complexity possible in the father-daughter relationship.
    (reflective, informative, persuasive)

2. Critics should recognize that the field of trauma studies could not exist without the works of Sylvia Plath.
    (reflective, informative, persuasive)

3. Sylvia Plath's relationship with poet Ted Hughes affected her later work deeply.
    (reflective, informative, persuasive)

4. No-kill animal shelters are finding creative ways to persuade people to adopt older pets.
    (reflective, informative, persuasive)

5. My experiences with Sylvester, a cat so old he was museum-quality, has given me a great fondness for elderly pets.
    (reflective, informative, persuasive)

6. The city should fine anyone who willfully abandons a pet.
    (reflective, informative, persuasive)

7. Lawmakers need to see that school vouchers will be the death of public schools.
    (reflective, informative, persuasive)

8. My parents, going against their friends' advice, sent me to a public school in the inner city. Their decision made a huge impact on how I, as an adult, feel about education.
    (reflective, informative, persuasive)

9. The voucher issue has set off a heated debate in both major political parties.
    (reflective, informative, persuasive)

10. The school voucher program has worked wonders for many at-risk kids. *(reflective, informative, persuasive)*

EXERCISE 3-5 *Creating the Thesis*

Write two summaries of the passage below. In the first summary, provide just the key points, as they appear. When you are done with this summary, rank the ideas in the order of their importance. For your second summary, focus on the top two ideas from your ranking and give more detail from the passage about these ideas. At the end of the second summary, explain why you decided this idea or these ideas were the most important. Finally, rewrite this explanation as one sentence—this is a thesis.

When two people talk, they don't just fall into physical and aural harmony. They also engage in what is called motor mimicry. If you show people pictures of a smiling face or a frowning face, they'll smile or frown back, although perhaps only in muscular changes so fleeting that they can only be captured with electronic sensors. If I hit my thumb with a hammer, most people watching will grimace: they'll mimic my emotional state. This is what is meant, in the technical sense, by empathy. We imitate each other's emotions as a way of expressing support and caring and, even more basically, as a way of communicating with each other.

—Malcolm Gladwell, *The Tipping Point: How Little Things Can Make a Big Difference*, 2000.

EXERCISE 3-6 *Evaluating the Thesis*

Here are several assignments and the thesis statement that a student has decided to use for that assignment. Evaluate these thesis statements according to their level of specificity, manageability, and interest. Then, rewrite each one to make them meet all three of the requirements.

1. Design a three-panel brochure intended to educate teenage boys about the responsibilities of fatherhood.
   Thesis: Think before having a baby. They are really expensive.

2. Write a three- to five-page paper for a child development class. The papers from this class will be published on a child-advocacy Web site.
   Thesis: Many formerly accepted methods of discipline are now considered child abuse.

3. Write a 10-15 page research paper on a revolutionary breakthrough in urban transportation to enter in a contest. Your paper will be evaluated by a panel of graduate students majoring in city planning.
Thesis: Washington D.C. has a great subway system called the Metro.

4. Write a 200- to 300-word article for a magazine geared towards 8-to 12-year-olds.
Thesis: It's never too early to start thinking about a career.

5. Write a one-page paper for your ethics class. You will use this paper to start class discussion.
Thesis: Reading employees' email is a violation of privacy.

EXERCISE 3-7 *For Practice: Writing the Outline*

Look again at the brainstorming list for Exercise 3-1, the freewrite you did for Exercise 3-3, or the summaries and thesis you extracted from the passage in Exercise 3-5. Choose one of these to pursue and write a short outline for a paper that includes three to five main topics.

EXERCISE 4-1 *Topic Sentences*

Find the topic sentence in each of the following paragraphs and underline it. If it is implied, write what you think it is on the line below.

1. I first got interested in the Civil War as a boy. Any Deep South boy, and probably all Southern boys, have been familiar with the Civil War as a sort of thing in their conscience going back. I honestly believe that it's in all our subconsciouses. This country was into its adolescence at the time of the Civil War. It really was; it hadn't formulated itself really as an adult nation, and the Civil War did that. Like all traumatic experiences that you might have had in your adolescence, it stays with you the rest of your life, constantly in your subconscious, most likely in your conscience, too.

   —Shelby Foote, in *Booknotes*, 1997

   _____

   _____

2. "NORM!" You want to go where everyone knows your name, right? Especially if it is a hip yuppie bar filled with good-looking and witty people. For years, television viewers tuned in to witness the antics of the crowd at "Cheers": Sam, Diane/Rebecca, Coach/Woody, Carla, Cliff and Norm, the corpulent resident of the corner stool. Frats even developed a drinking game in which each participant had to down a shot every time Norm was greeted by the other regulars. Here comes the regular, and, as the Replacements song goes, "am I the only one to feel ashamed" that both the viewing public and the media celebrate an alcoholic television character?

   _____

   _____

3. When was the last time you were in the mood for a nice, hearty, basic meal and the only thing that would do was a heaping plate of spaghetti and meatballs? It would have to be about every other day for me. Sometimes, though, a nice light chicken dish with some bread and herb butter would hit the spot. Enter Al Capone's Ristorante Italiano. This little joint on Barton Springs Road is a haven for those who enjoy good home-cooked Italian food and a peaceful atmosphere. When Tex-Mex, Chinese, or steak won't do, Al Capone's proves that it is by far the best place to go for Italian food.

---

4. The "official" Web site produced by gwbush.com titled www.gwbush.com: *Hypocrisy with Bravado* is a direct parody of the Web sites put out by various Republican party affiliates. Unlike those "official" sites, however, *gwbush.com* is not intended for supporters of George W. Bush's campaign for president but rather voters who are bemused by this front-runner's hypocrisy. By using humor to make a very serious point—voters need to be outraged by the hypocrisy of our potential leaders—*gwbush.com* reaches out effectively to not only those voters who are anti-Bush, but to the general public who needs to be made aware of this issue.

EXERCISE 4-2 *Organizing Paragraphs*

A student is writing a paper on Bobby Sands, a member of the IRA who was the first to die during a 1981 hunger strike in a British prison. The strikers wanted political rather than regular criminal status within the prison. The student has the following ideas for paragraphs. Which of the seven common organization strategies would work best for each?

1. Conditions within a British prison, circa 1980.
   *Organizational strategy*_____

2. History of the hunger strike as a political tool.
   Organizational strategy _____

3. Treatment of criminal status prisoners and political status prisoners.
   Organizational strategy _____

4. What political status is.
   Organizational strategy _____

5. The evolution of the strike.
   Organizational strategy _____

6. The popularity of Bobby Sands and the other strikers.
   Organizational strategy _____

7. Breakdown of the Catholic population in Derry, Northern Ireland, and of the Catholic prison population
   Organizational strategy _____

EXERCISE 4-3 *For Practice: Organizational Strategy*

Find a paper you wrote either for this class or for another class. Choose one paragraph and rewrite it, organizing it according to one of the strategies from this section. Make sure you choose a strategy that is different from the one you used when you first wrote the paragraph!

EXERCISE 4-4 *Reiterating and Transitional Terms*

Rewrite these paragraphs using the two strategies mentioned in Section 4c to make them cohere. Use each strategy at least once. Note that one of the paragraphs has incorporated one of the strategies, but has done so poorly.

1. Three kids go into the woods to seek out an evil witch who lives in a remote cabin. They lose their way and run out of food. Something mysterious happens when they finally meet the witch. Does this sound familiar? It is the plot to many familiar fairy tales. It is the plot to the blockbuster film, The Blair Witch Project.

2. In fairy tales from many different cultures, the woods tend to represent a variety of psychological forces. It can represent the dark side of the individual soul, the id. From a social standpoint, the lack of civilization or culture is represented. Most of all, there's a loss of

innocence. Children who are in the transition to adulthood are cast out, and must find their way. They must also battle a force out there that robs them of their innocence. If they survive the journey there, they come back to civilization as adults.

3. The woods are also a liminal space. Magical and impossible things happen in the woods. Creatures can adopt roles opposite their nature. Animals can speak. Mortal enemies can be friends. In Through the Looking Glass, Alice encounters a baby deer in the woods. She and the deer become friends. They gain comfort from one another. They reach the end of the woods. The deer looks at Alice and recognizes her as its enemy, man. The deer runs away in fright.

4. The college students in *The Blair Witch Project*, one could argue, are in an arrested state of development, as are many college students. Like children, they are titillated by the stories that the locals tell them about the Blair Witch. Like adolescents, they believe that they know it all. In this adolescent state, they mock the locals' superstitions and they mock the Blair Witch. They behave in an adolescent fashion; the girl is bossy and demanding. The boys respond as adolescents, and do things to spite the girl's carefully detailed plans. One boy throws the map away. The other begins to behave erratically, and starts to act out physically. In the movie it seems as if the boys' adolescent behavior is being caused by the Blair Witch. It could be argued that they are just handling the transition from adolescence to adulthood very poorly.

EXERCISE 4-5 *For Practice: Signaling Relationships with Transitional Terms*

Choose a paragraph from a paper you have written for either this class or another class. Underline any transitional words or phrases you used and mark spaces where you think you need a transitional word or phrase. Write out the relationship expressed by the transitions you underlined. Then, write out the relationship that needs to be expressed in each place that you marked. What transitional word or phrase could you add to make that relationship clear?

EXERCISE 4-6 *For Practice: Coherence*

Find a paper that you've written either for this or another class. Choose a paper that has more than five paragraphs, if possible. Write out the first sentence of each paragraph. Does this list of first sentences tell a coherent story? Mark the places where one sentence links to the next. Did you use a transition? Repetition? If you used a transition, underline it and write out the relationship being expressed. If you used repetition, underline the word or idea being repeated.

Now, mark the places where the sentences do not connect. Write out the relationship that needs to be expressed and the best method to achieve this, repetition or transition. If repetition, write what word or idea needs to be repeated. If you need a transition, write what relationship needs to be addressed and the word or phrase that would best achieve this.

EXERCISE 4-7 *Writing Effective Beginning and Ending Paragraphs*

Write an introductory and a concluding paragraph for each of the essays described below. Label what each paragraph does from the lists in Section 4f: asks a question, makes a recommendation.

1. An essay explaining the process for applying to colleges.
2. A description of a moment when you completely changed your mind about a person.
3. A proposal to make talking on a cell phone while driving a felony.
4. An analysis of a short story, poem, or novel by your favorite author.
5. A letter to the editor of a newspaper or magazine responding to an article, editorial, letter, or advertisement you felt was misinformed or inappropriate, or that presented a viewpoint that opposes your opinion on a subject.

Chapter 5

Rewriting, Editing, and Proofreading

EXERCISE 5-1 *Responding to Drafts*

Read the following rough draft and respond, following the process outlined in Section 5c. Resist the urge to edit sentences and correct mechanical errors.

We've Come Along Way, Baby

Humans has existed on the Earth for approximately 3.4 million years. That's from when the oldest human ancestor, ""Lucy," an Australopithecus, discovered by Donald Johnson and M. Taieb. s had been found. Lucy was not only the oldest Australopithecus find, they also found over 40% of her skeleton intact, making her one of the most complete, too. Australopithecus africanus, means "southern ape from Africa" (Lewin).

Australopithecine's looked more like primates than modern-day Homo Sapiens. Although they walked upright, they had low, sloping foreheads, protruding jaws, and thick body hair. They were also only about three feet tall. For some reason, they also didn't seem to show any facial expressions (McKie 50).

Humans have evolved a lot over the past three and a half million years. We are almost 6 feet, have lost most of our body hair, have adapted to walking upright all the time, and we've grown brains that are over three times as large as the first Australopithecine's (Larson 123). Besides, humans (Homo Sapiens) have also developed an advanced material culture. We live in cities now and we don't have to live in trees. We also don't have to dig in the ground for our food; we can just buy it at the store. We also can grasp abstract concepts like time and we have art and literature.

But we haven't changed all that much, really. We still are related to primates in many ways. This can be seen in the way our hands, feet, and over all body is structured. Our faces are even very similar (IHO).

There have been four distinct species of human throughout time: Homo Habilis, Homo Erectus, Homo sapiens Neanderthalesis, and Homo sapiens Sapiens. The first major step in evolution was becoming bipedal, or walking upright (Larson 20). As I said before, Australopithecine's were the first to do this. They were really clumsy, though; because their skeleton weren't really able to support the weight, they probably spent most of their time on all fours. They were, however, probably really good at climbing trees. This is not the only way they were more similar to primates than homo sapiens, though (McKie 35). They were tiny, with a tiny (orange size) brain, prominent cheekbones, and thick molars. Like chimps, they had small, underdeveloped thumbs. But their toes were shorter than other primates (IHO).

Australiopithicene also probably lived socailly like chimps. Judging from the way fossils were at their sites, they probably lived in one place in small groups. We think they lived in groups because usually about 5 individuals are found in the same place. One site even had had 13 in the same place! (Lewin) Scientists think that these groups usually had one male in charge and this was because of their sexual dimorphism. Sexual dimorphism, or the difference in size between the genders, usually means that males are larger (Lewin). So probably the one guy that was big was in charge.

They also weren't very smart. The only tools they had were sticks and rocks. They were also vegetarians. They may not have known animals could be eaten. If they did know, though, they probably couldn't figure out how to kill one anyway. Homo Habilis, though, figured this out (Larson 145). Homo Habilis is the earliest known member of the Homo genus, and has been found only in Africa. Homo Habilis's brain was about 50% larger than Australopithecine's, he was taller, had flatter nostrils, and their faces were nearly hairless (IHO).

Most importantly, though, Homo Habilis figured out, through scavenging, scientists think, that meat was edible. Their teeth show that they started to add meat to their vegetarian diets. Homo Habilis lived in Africa until about 1.6 million years ago, when Homo Erectus emerged, causing their eventual extinction. Homo Erectus was the next step. He had a much larger brain (1060 cc) than Homo Habilis (Mc Kie 80). "Homo Erectus" means "Man who Walks Upright" (Lewin).

The larger brain is the main physical change from H. Hablis to Homo Erectus. But they did have smaller jaws and teeth. They also had a larger brow. The brow-ridge was also slightly larger than Homo Habilis. "The term Homo habilis means handy man, a name selected for the deposits of primitive tools found near H. habilis fossils (Lewin).

Homo Erectus lived until about 100,000 years ago, when Homo sapiens Neanderthalesis took over. Homo sapiens Neanderthalesis, or the Neanderthals, lived during the most recent Ice Age (Larson 160).

Evolution happens so slowly that it almost can't be seen. The changes occur in tiny mutations; if you possess a mutation that makes you survive better than others, you are more likely to reproduce and spread that mutation into the next generation. If you have a bad mutation, you die and you don't pass that mutation on. There are lots of examples that prove this, from the problems in royal families to skin color differences that are related to climate (Larson 30).

We have to remember, though, that all of these things are just physical. Deep down, all humans are really the same so we should love and respect one another.

Works Cited

Institute of Human Origins (IHO). Becoming Human. 2001. 23 February 2002 <http://www.becominghuman.org/>.

Larsen, Clark Spencer, and Robert M. Matter. Human Origins : The Fossil Record. Waveland Press, 1998.

Lewin, Roger. "Australopithecines," Microsoft® Encarta® Encyclopedia 99. 1998.

--. "Homo habilis," Microsoft® Encarta® Encyclopedia 99.

McKie, Robin. The Dawn of Man: The Story of Human Evolution. London: DK, 2002.

EXERCISE 5-2 *For Practice: Responding*

Exchange drafts of a paper for this class or for another with another student. Respond to this student's paper following the procedure underlined in section 5c. Resist the urge to edit sentences and correct mechanical errors.

Chapter 6

Critical Reading and Viewing

EXERCISE 6-1 *Fallacies*

Build a collection of fallacies. See if you can find examples of all thirteen fallacies mentioned in section 6c. Make sure you cite the source of your fallacy. Create examples for the ones you can't find. Compare your examples with those of your classmates.

EXERCISE 6-2 *Critical Viewing*

Find an interesting photo in your textbook, a magazine, or newspaper. Write a brief (one- or two-page) analysis of this photo following the process outlined in Section 6d. Pay particular attention to the last question: "After you have thought about this picture, how has your first impression changed?"

EXERCISE 6-3 *Visual Fallacies/Misleading Images*

Altered photos can have a huge impact, especially when they rewrite history, or are used to "prove" the existence of some otherworldly beast. (See the example of the Gardner Civil War photo and story in Section 6e.) Faced with such grand hoaxes, though, we often overlook the prevalence of altered images in our daily lives. Find an image that has clearly been altered in an advertisement, on TV (you can write a description of the image and cite the source), on the Internet or in the newspaper (newspapers like the *National Inquirer* and *Weekly World News* routinely alter images). Write a few paragraphs about this image. What has been altered? Is the producer of the image up front about the alteration? What, do you think, was the purpose behind the alteration of this photo? What are the possible implications?

EXERCISE 6-4 *For Practice*

Advertising has become so much a part of our lives that we are very nearly blind to its more subtle manifestations. Look around your room; how many corporate logos and brand names do you see? Make a list of all that you find and compare with others in your class. Are you surprised by the results?

Chapter 7
Analyzing Verbal and Visual Texts

EXERCISE 7-1 *Develop and Organize a Rhetorical Analysis*

Public speeches are usually intended to persuade. You can find many examples of public speeches on the Web. Many politically oriented Web sites contain transcripts of speeches and often the audio and video. (For example, go to www.whitehouse.gov for speeches by the President.) Select a speech to analyze and answer the following questions:

1. What is the *rhetorical purpose*? What did the speech intend to achieve?

2. Where was the speech given? How does the speaker connect with the beliefs and attitudes of the *audience*?

3. What appeals does the speech rely upon: the *rational* appeal (logos), the *emotional* appeal (pathos), or the *ethical* appeal (ethos)?

4. How is the speech *organized*?

5. How formal or informal is the *style*? Is humor used?

6. Does the speaker use any *metaphors* and for what purpose?

When you complete your analysis, formulate a *thesis* about the speech.

EXERCISE 7-2 *Analyze Images and Other Kinds of Visual Texts*

The leaders of classical Rome were keenly aware of the persuasive power of public building and monuments. In addition to statues and columns, Romans built arches to commemorate emperors and military victories. Visitors and citizens of Rome alike were reminded of the power of Imperial Rome when they walked under an arch. The massive size of the arch suggested the might and majesty of Rome while the intricate decorative details commemorated specific military conquests and the triumphs celebrated afterward.

Find an example of public architecture in your city or town. What messages does it convey? What do you think the designers and city leaders had in mind when they built it?

Chapter 8
Writing to Reflect

EXERCISE 8-1 *Reflecting*

Look at your immediate workspace. Are you at home, at the library, at a coffee house or elsewhere? If you are someplace that is familiar to you, list the first five people that this place makes you think about, the first five things this place makes you think about, and the first five events in your past that you associate with this place. Can you connect any of these into a brief narrative? Write a one-paragraph narrative of a memory this place inspires, using the items from your lists.

If the place isn't familiar to you, choose an object, person or aspect of the atmosphere that reminds you of something else. Does the smell of the coffee bring back a memory? Does the person napping across the table from you at the library remind you of anyone? Use your moment now to frame a memory you could associate with this particular place.

EXERCISE 8-2 *Identifying Focus*

Find a short reflective piece of writing in the newspaper, a magazine, a book, etc. or on the Internet. Many popular magazines, for example, have articles in which celebrities detail their story of a marital break-up, illness, bouts with depression or addiction, or other personal details. Talk shows and interviews are also ripe for this sort of personal narrative. Write a paragraph in which you analyze the format of the message: does the intended purpose actually line up with the way in which the message is presented and with its intended audience?

EXERCISE 8-3 *Developing a Response*

Return to the paragraph you wrote for Exercise 8-1. Develop this paragraph into a full response using the advice provided in Section 7c. Find a focus for your response, and add details to make the reflection come alive for the reader. Remember to give your response an attention-getting introduction and a thoughtful conclusion.

EXERCISE 8-4 *For Practice*

Visit a local museum or event, see an exhibit, watch a documentary, or listen to a radio program that claims to present the "true" story of something that is central to your identity—your ethnicity, your community, your social group, your sexual orientation, your hometown, your socio-economic class, your religion, for example. Write a magazine-style reflection on your experience, using Sylvia's essays as a model. Take photographs, if possible, or use other images to support your text. Remember to stay focused, keep the information organized, and provide vivid details. You must also cite any sources you use (museum information, the documentary you watch, the radio program you listen to, etc.) and get permission from anyone you might interview or photograph.

Chapter 9

Writing to Inform

EXERCISE 9-1 *Finding an Informative Topic*

Informative writing in college often involves explaining a concept. Pick a particular academic discipline that interests you (psychology, government, biology, art) or another broad subject area (the environment, college athletics, eating disorders). List at least five central concepts for that discipline or area of interest. When you finish, review your list and select one concept as a possible topic.

Take five minutes to write what you know about that concept. Why does it interest you? What more would you like to know about it?

Next, make a quick survey of information about the concept. If your library has online resources such as specialized encyclopedias, look up the concept, or else go to the library. Do a Web search using a search engine. After an hour or two, you should know if you can find enough information to write about this concept.

EXERCISE 9-2 *Sharpening Focus*

An informative thesis statement should contain the topic and indicate your particular focus. To sharpen that focus, answer the following questions:

1. Who are your readers? What are they likely to know about your topic?

2. What makes you interested in this topic?

3. What are the major subdivisions of your topic? Which one or ones are you writing about?

4. What key words are important to your topic?

Look at your thesis statement and your answers to the questions. Revise your thesis statement to include a sharper focus.

EXERCISE 9-3 *Organization*

Which of the organizations discussed in Section 8c would work best for each of the following topics?

1. how to interview for a job
2. the unseen stresses faced by teenaged girls
3. an analysis of the causes of the Spanish-American War
4. a description of Egyptian burial practices
5. how to install software on a computer
6. a comparison of two different proposals to solve the same problem
7. a description of the Battle of the Little Bighorn
8. an analysis of the rhetorical styles of Malcolm X and Martin Luther King, Jr.
9. an analysis of a proposal to make a course in English grammar mandatory for all entering freshmen
10. a continent-by-continent survey of the various styles of Stone Age cave painting

EXERCISE 9-4 *Creating an Informative Essay*

An informative essay can do several things. It can report information; analyze meaning, patterns and connections; explain how to do something; and explore questions or problems.

Write a 3-5 page informative essay using one of the following questions to help you formulate your thesis.

1. What (or who) is X?
2. How does X work?
3. What are the different opinions on X?
4. What caused X?
5. What effects has X had?

Use the sample essay in the previous section as a model. Ask your instructor what format you should use for your citations.

EXERCISE 9-5 *For Practice*

Working with a group of two or three other students, create an informative brochure. You can choose as your subject a service, business, or organization located on campus or in the local community. Use the advice given in the section to help you format your brochure. Make sure you clearly identify your audience, your purpose, and your context before you get started.

EXERCISE 10-1 *Arguable Claims*

Which of the following statements are arguable claims? Which are statements of fact, personal taste, or claims of belief? If a statement seems borderline, how could it be made into an arguable claim?

1. The United States has by far the highest rate of deaths by handguns.

   _____

   _____

   _____

2. Individuals should not be allowed to own handguns.

   _____

   _____

   _____

3. *Lord of the Rings* is the best fantasy movie ever made.

   _____

   _____

   _____

4. Buddhism is superior to other religions because it considers that the root of evil lies in craving—both sensual pleasures and material possessions.

   _____

   _____

   _____

5. Buddhism began in India in the sixth century BCE.

_____

_____

_____

6. Graffiti should be considered art and not vandalism.

_____

_____

_____

7. Any sport performed to music is not really a sport and should be not be included in the Olympics.

_____

_____

_____

EXERCISE 10-2 *Make an Arguable Claim*

Collect five slogans from advertisements, posters, the news, T-shirts, even bumper stickers. Expand each slogan into a potential proposal argument by brainstorming evidence that will answer the challenges So what? Why? and How?

EXERCISE 10-3 *Develop and Organize Good Reasons*

Return to your slogans from Exercise 10-2. Choose one that is particularly interesting or that presents a wealth of possible arguments. Try to come up with a thesis based on the slogan for each line of argument (definition, value, comparison/contrast, consequence).

EXERCISE 10-4 *Argument*

Using one of the slogan theses you developed in Exercise 10-3, the list of topics you generated for Exercise 3.1, or a topic from Yahoo's Issues and Causes Web page, write a thesis that follows one of the lines of argument. Write a complete argument for it. Follow the structure outlined in Section 10c and use the paper in Section 10d as a model.

To make sure you address possible rebuttals, exchange papers with another student and develop counterarguments for each other's arguments.

EXERCISE 10-5 *A Persuasive Letter of Application and Résumé*

Find a job listing in the newspaper or on your school's job database that you would consider applying for. Write a letter of application and a résumé that would make you a strong candidate. Do not, however, pad your résumé with false or misleading information.

EXERCISE 11-1 *Designing a Flyer*

Following is a flyer for a German Club party. Are the graphics and text effective? Are they attractive? Make a list of suggestions for improving both the flyer's look and its readability.

SPRECHEN SIE DEUTSCH?
Would you like to learn?

Wo? (Where?): Ye Olde Tavern, 1930 Park St.
Wann? (When?): 8:30 P.M. Friday, March 1
Mit Wem? (With Whom?): University German Club
Warum? (Why?): To speak German, learn how you can if you can't, make friends!
CALL 212-8080 FOR MORE INFORMATION

Chapter 12

Illustrations, Tables, and Charts

EXERCISE 12-1 *Deciding on Graphics*

Decide what kind of graphic (photo, drawing, table, bar graph, line graph, pie chart, or flow chart) would best represent the information listed below. In some cases, there might be more than one correct answer.

1. At the time of first European contact, North and South America was inhabited by an estimated 90 million people. There were about 10 million in America north of present-day Mexico; 30 million in Mexico; 11 million in Central America; 445,000 in the Caribbean islands; and 39 million in South America.
   Type of graphic:_____

2. The estimated date of the earliest migrations into the Americas is about 30,000 years ago. Bone tools have been discovered in the Yukon, however, that have been radiocarbon-dated to 22,000 BC and campfire remains in central Mexico, have been radiocarbon-dated to 21,000 BC. In a cave in the Andes Mountains of Peru, archaeologists have found stone tools and butchered animal bones that have been dated to 18,000 BC. A cave in Idaho, in the United States, contains similar items, dated to 12,500 BC.
   *Type of graphic:*_____

3. The social, political, or economic organization of the Cherokee nation.
   *Type of graphic:*_____

4. The similarities and differences in regard to language, social structure, economy, and culture between the Five Civilized Tribes: the Cherokee, the Choctaw, the Chickasaw, the Creek, and the Seminole.
   *Type of graphic:*_____

5. The differences in the shelters built by Native American groups living in the ten culture areas of North America (the Southwest, the Eastern Woodlands, the Southeast, the Plains, the California-Intermountain region, the Plateau, the Subarctic, the Northwest Pacific Coast, and the Arctic).
   *Type of graphic:*_____

6. The number of expeditions to the Americas undertaken per year by European nations.
   *Type of graphic:*_____

7. The internal structure of a Moche pyramid.
   *Type of graphic:*_____

8. The size of Native American societies in relation to the amount of food available.
   *Type of graphic:*_____

9. The qualities of the many varieties of maize grown by Native Americans.
   *Type of graphic:*_____

10. The percentage of different tribes that make up the population of Native Americans living in the United States today.
    *Type of graphic:*_____

Chapter 13
Verbal and Visual Presentations

EXERCISE 13-1 *For Practice: Oral Presentations*

Think about an oral presentation you have recently seen—class lectures, presentations at work, public talks, etc.—and choose both the one that you felt was the most effective and the one that you felt was the least effective. Using examples from these presentations, create a list of effective tactics and a list of ineffective or poor tactics.

EXERCISE 13-2 *For Practice: Oral and Visual Presentations*

Choose an informative or persuasive paper you have written for either this class or for another class and rework it as an oral presentation. Rewrite the language of your paper to be heard rather than read. Add visuals where necessary or organize your talk with presentation software. Insert anecdotes or some humor where appropriate.

Practice your talk with a group of classmates and get feedback on your material, your visuals, your speaking manner, and on your body language. If possible, videotape the practice so that you can do a self-critique.

Chapter 14
Writing for the Web

EXERCISE 14-1 *Evaluating Web Sites*

Make two lists. On one list, write out the Web sites you always enjoy visiting and explain why. Are they updated frequently? Easy to navigate? Quick to load? Do they act as indexes to other useful sites? What else do you like about them?

On the other list, write out the Web sites that you often have to visit but always find annoying or frustrating. Explain why—are they slow to load? Do the applications "crash" your computer? Are they frequently out of date? Are they hard to navigate? What else do you find frustrating about these sites?

EXERCISE 14-2 *For Practice: Audience and Purpose, Content, Readability, Visual Design, and Navigation*

Choose a Web site that you are very familiar with and write a brief evaluation of it. Keep notes focusing on the five points below:

1. Audience and purpose
2. Content
3. Readability
4. Visual Design
5. Navigation

See Writing in the World in Chapter 14, for further explanation of these points.

Chapter 15
Planning Your Research

EXERCISE 15-1 *Research Strategy*

Determine the strategy required for each of the following assignment topics: analysis/examination, review of scholarship, survey, evaluation, or argument.

1. How does the student body feel about the proposed raise in tuition?
   (analysis/examination, review of scholarship, survey, evaluation or argument)

2. What do scientists know about the effectiveness of acupuncture in treating various forms of addiction?
   (analysis/examination, review of scholarship, survey, evaluation or argument)

3. How historically accurate is the film *Gladiator*?
   (analysis/examination, review of scholarship, survey, evaluation or argument)

4. What caused the crash of the technology market in 2000?
   (analysis/examination, review of scholarship, survey, evaluation or argument)

5. How far should the government go to prevent terrorism?
   (analysis/examination, review of scholarship, survey, evaluation or argument)

EXERCISE 15-2 *Finding a Topic*

Think of a general topic you might write about for one of your courses (the human genome, the European Union, pragmatism, the National Parks, the Negro Leagues of baseball, etc.) Then, gather lists of subtopics using a Web directory, a general encyclopedia, and a specialized encyclopedia (if applicable). Answer the questions that follow.

1. What subtopics do all of the resources provide for this general topic?
2. Do any of the subtopics lead to other subtopics? Which ones?

3. Which resource produced the most useful list of subtopics for this general topic?
4. Which of the subtopics generated seems the most fruitful to pursue? Why?

EXERCISE 15-3 *Developing A Working Thesis*

Choose one of the subtopics you found for Exercise 15-2 to develop into a research project. Do some preliminary research on this topic and develop a topic, research question, and working thesis, using the advice given in Section 15d.

Topic:

Research question:

Working thesis:

EXERCISE 15-4 *Primary and Secondary Research*

What kind of research (primary, secondary, or both) would each of the topics listed below require?

1. the programs a local public radio station should add or remove from its schedule
   (*primary, secondary, or both*)

2. the history of the color line in American sports
   (*primary, secondary, or both*)

3. how people applying for unemployment could be better served
   (*primary, secondary, or both*)

4. the emotional, physical, and social health of children raised by same-sex parents
   (*primary, secondary, or both*)

5. Japanese *manga* (comic strip narratives) as a working-class art form
   (*primary, secondary, or both*)

Chapter 16

Finding Print Sources in Libraries

EXERCISE 16-1 *Libraries and/or Internet*

Decide where (library, Internet, or both) you might find each of the items below. If you could find it in both the library and on the Internet, what are the advantages of one over the other?

1. *Jay's Journal of Anomalies*, by Ricky Jay
   (*library, Internet, or both*)
2. reviews of *Jay's Journal of Anomalies*
   (*library, Internet, or both*)
3. an interview with author Ricky Jay
   (*library, Internet, or both*)
4. a newspaper article from the nineteenth century that describes a magician's performance
   (*library, Internet, or both*)
5. the 2001 membership roster for the International Brotherhood of Magicians
   (*library, Internet, or both*)
6. a comprehensive history of the American sideshow
   (*library, Internet, or both*)
7. the current auction value of several pieces of magic memorabilia
   (*library, Internet, or both*)
8. the date of Penn and Teller's next television appearance
   (*library, Internet, or both*)
9. the number of books published about Harry Houdini one year after his death
   (*library, Internet, or both*)
10. the etymology of the word *mesmerize*
    (*library, Internet, or both*)

EXERCISE 16-2 *Identify Keywords*

Formulate a research question and write a working thesis (see Section 15d). Underline the main concepts in your working thesis. Put each concept at the top of a column. Under each concept write as many words or phrases that you can think of that describe the concept or are associated with the concept.

EXERCISE 16-3 *Periodicals*

Decide what kind of periodical (trade, popular, scholarly) you would turn to for information on each of the topics listed below.

1. results of a recent study on the long-term physiological effects of Prozac
   (trade, popular, scholarly)

2. a first-person account of one woman's experiences with depression
   (trade, popular, scholarly)

3. a review of a self-help book titled *Be Your Own Therapist*
   (trade, popular, scholarly)

4. an essay arguing that Mary Shelley's *Frankenstein* was heavily influenced by the author's struggles with depression
   (trade, popular, scholarly)

5. a description of a new reading skills program for students with mild learning disabilities
   (trade, popular, scholarly)

EXERCISE 16-4 *Creating a Bibliography*

Create note cards or computer files for a potential topic for research. Make sure you have the complete bibliographical information for each source. Here is an example entry in MLA format:

> Lee, J.J. *Ireland 1912-1985: Politics and Society.* New York: Cambridge U.P., 1989.

Refer to Chapters 21-25 for MLA, APA, Chicago, and CBE formats. Ask your instructor which format you should use for this exercise.

Chapter 17
Finding Sources Online

EXERCISE 17-1 *Find Articles and Other Sources in Library Databases*

Find five databases on your library's Web site. If you are unsure where to find databases, visit your library and talk to a reference librarian. Use two or three keywords as search terms (see section 16b). Compare the results. Which database turned up more results? Which turned up more scholarly journals? Which turned up more popular journals and newspapers?

EXERCISE 17-2 *Using Search Engines*

A recent search on Google using the phrase "hate crimes" resulted in the following URLs. Answer the questions that follow with the letter of the correct URL. Use only the clues provided by the URLs to answer the questions.

A. http://www.fbi.gov/publish/hatecrime.htm

B. http://www.ncjrs.org/hate_crimes/hate_crimes.html

C. http://unquietmind.com/hate_crime.html

D. http://caag.state.ca.us/civilrights/content/hatecrimes.htm

E. http://www.infoplease.com/spot/hatecrimes.html

F. http://www.xq.com/cuav.hatecr1.htm

1. On which of the sites are you most likely to find advertisements? *Correct URL_____*

2. Which site is most likely to feature the opinions of an individual? *Correct URL_____*

3. Which site is most likely to provide you with information on hate crime legislation in California? *Correct URL_____*

4. Which site probably contains out-of-date information? *Correct URL_____*

5. Which site is probably funded by grants from the government or public donations? *Correct URL*_____

6. Which site is provides information from the federal government? *Correct URL*_____

Chapter 18

Evaluating Sources

EXERCISE 18-1 *Evaluating for Relevance and Reliability*

Return to the working bibliography you wrote for Exercise 16.4. Using the advice given in Chapter 18, evaluate your sources for relevance and reliability. Do any of your sources pose potential problems? Are there still ways you can use them in your argument?

EXERCISE 18-2 *Relevance and Reliability*

Here is a working bibliography that uses a few of the sources from Exercise 17-2. Evaluate these sources as if you would be using them for a research paper dealing with hate crime legislation in Texas. Answer these two questions for each:

- How relevant is this source (very, somewhat, slightly, not at all)? Why?
- How reliable is this source (very, somewhat, slightly, not at all)? See guidelines given in sections 18b and 18c.

1. United States. Federal Bureau of Investigation. Hate Crime Statistics. 2002. 17 Sept. 2002. <http://www.fbi.gov/ucr/cius_00/hate00.pdf>.

   Government site distributing hate crime statistics. The most recent statistics available are for 2000.

2. "Governor Of Texas Signs New Hate Crime Bill." Jet. 28 May 2001: 16.

   Short article (262 words) about Governor Perry signing the James Byrd Jr. Hate Crime Act.

3. Spong, John. "The Hate Debate." Texas Monthly. April 2001. 10 February 2002. <http://web.lexis-nexis.com/universe/document>

   Long article (2216 words) dealing specifically with the controversy over hate crime legislation in Texas.

4. Levin, Jack, and Jack McDevitt. Hate Crimes: The Rising Tide of Bigotry and Bloodshed . Boulder, CO: Westview Press, 2001.

   Scholarly study of the causes of the recent increase in hate crimes in the U.S.

5. National Criminal Justice Referral Service. In the Spotlight: Hate Crimes. 2001. 17 Sept. 2002
    <http://www.ncjrs.org/hate_crimes/hate_crimes.html>

    Site for a non-profit organization affiliated with the Department of Justice. The site is a clearinghouse for various forms of information about hate crimes (statistics, legal information, reports, links to other sites, etc.)

Chapter 19

Avoiding Plagiarism When Using Sources

EXERCISE 19-1 *Determining Plagiarism*

Below is a list of situations. Decide which are instances of plagiarism or scholastic dishonesty and which are not.

1. You cut and paste information from a Web site into your notes for an economics paper that is due tomorrow. Unfortunately, you lose track of what information is quoted directly, what is paraphrased, and what is summarized. You do your best to sort out which ideas are yours and which came from the Web site, but you don't have time to check everything out before your paper is due. _____

2. A paper for a required government course is due on the same day that a really important paper for a core class in your major is due. You borrow a paper from your roommate, but you rewrite it in your own words and you hand it in. _____

3. A passage in your English paper is a paraphrase of a lecture your history instructor gave. Your English instructor did not require you to use any outside sources, so you do not create a Works Cited sheet for the paper. _____

4. You are in a real crunch for time, so your friend, an English major, edits your paper. She rewrites a few awkward sentences and corrects a few of your facts. You type in her changes before turning in the paper. _____

5. You scan a picture from the cover of a CD to put on your personal Web site. Everyone knows where the picture came from, so you don't cite the source. _____

EXERCISE 19-2 *Using Citations*

Which of the following pieces of information require a citation and which do not?

1. Elvis Presley was born in Tupelo, Mississippi on January 8, 1935.

   _____

2. Peter Guralnick wrote *Last Train to Memphis*, which chronicles Elvis's youth in Tupelo, Mississippi and Memphis, Tennessee.

_____

3. In this book, Guralnick tries to present as complete a picture as possible of Elvis as a teenager, and not as the superstar he was to become. _____

4. Frank Sinatra thought that Elvis's music inspired destructive behavior in young people. _____

5. Critics denounce Elvis for stealing the style, rhythms, and, in some cases, the actual lyrics of black music, but many black artists, like Jackie Wilson, felt that this was not the case.

_____

6. Graceland, Elvis Presley's former home, is in Memphis.

_____

7. On December 31, 1956, the *Wall Street Journal* reported that sales of Elvis Presley memorabilia had grossed over $22 million in the past few months. _____

8. Elvis's mother, Gladys, died on August 14, 1958.

_____

9. Friends and family say that Elvis and his mother shared a special bond that made others, including Elvis's father Vernon, feel like outsiders. _____

10. Elvis Presley died at Graceland on August 16, 1977.

_____

EXERCISE 19-3 *Using Quotes*

Below are excerpts from two sources and a passage that incorporates quotations from both. Rewrite the paragraph, correcting punctuation and citation errors.

Source #1: Brice, Chris. "Literary Illusion?" The Advertiser. 9 Feb. 2002: M20.

American author Armistead Maupin''s latest novel [*The Night Listener*] is tangled up in the divide between truth and fiction, and not even he can be sure which is which. It centers around the bizarre story of Anthony Godby Johnson, the boy author of a best-selling book who was once described as "the bravest teen in America." [. . .]

[...] Maupin is just one of many thousands of people who have been moved by Tony Johnson's 1993 memoir, A Rock and a Hard Place, published when Johnson was just 15 years old, and telling of a life of horrific physical and sexual abuse. [. . .]

[. . .] Maupin now says *The Night Listener* was not entirely "a fanciful concoction on the part of a novelist with a far too vivid imagination, but was drawn from his own experiences of the "real-life Hitchcockian mystery of Tony Johnson."

Source #2: Friend, Tad. "Virtual Love." The New Yorker. 26 Nov. 2001.

[. . .] Tony has become a symbol of modern victimhood, his body torn apart by the most appalling end-of-the millennium traumas—child abuse and AIDS. (88) [. . .]

[. . .]When I visited Maupin again recently, I noticed that he had removed Tony's picture from his living room. But he told me, "Tony's still more real to me than many people who demonstrably do exist. I wrote the ending of the book the way I'd like it to be in life, because I'd have great trouble killing that child in my head." (99)

Essay:

Tony Johnson, child survivor of abuse and AIDS as well as the author of the best-selling book *A Rock and A Hard Place*, has a problem. Many of his celebrity friends don't believe he exists. One of the most outspoken of these friends is Armistead Maupin, who is one of many thousands of people who have been moved by Tony Johnson's 1993 memoir. But why have so many people been taken in by this boy author? According to Friend, "Tony has become a symbol of modern victimhood, his body torn apart by the most appalling end-of-the millennium traumas—child abuse and AIDS." No one, however, has ever met Tony Johnson.

After a series of events that caused him to doubt Tony's existence, Maupin wrote the novel, *The Night Listener*, in which the lives of characters Donna and Pete bear a striking resemblance to that of Tony and his adopted mother, Vicki Johnson. The novel was published in 2000 and was met with instant controversy. Maupin, however, afraid that Tony still might actually exist, insisted that the story was "a fanciful concoction on the part of a novelist with a far too vivid imagination."

("Literary" 20) Later, he admitted that the book was inspired by his own experiences as a character in the real-life Hitchcockian mystery of Tony Johnson (Friend 20). However, the novel and its controversial story line do not signify that Maupin bears Tony, whoever or whatever he may be, any ill will. Quite the contrary:

"When I visited Maupin again recently, I noticed that he had removed Tony's picture from his living room. But he told me, "Tony's still more real to me than many people who demonstrably do exist. I wrote the ending of the book the way I'd like it to be in life, because I'd have great trouble killing that child in my head."

To this day, no one really knows if Tony Johnson ever existed.

EXERCISE 19-4 *Using Paraphrases*

Two sources dealing with Abraham Lincoln and his association in American pop culture with the log cabin are excerpted below. Decide if the numbered paraphrases and summaries of the two sources are correct. If not, rewrite.

Source #1: "Lincoln, Abraham," Microsoft Encarta Encyclopedia 99. 1993-1998. Microsoft Corporation.

In December 1808 the Lincolns moved to a 141-hectare (348-acre) farm on the south fork of Nolin Creek near what is now Hodgenville, Kentucky. On February 12, 1809, in a log cabin that Thomas Lincoln had built, a son, Abraham, was born. Later the Lincolns had a second son who died in infancy. [. . .]

In the winter of 1816 the Lincolns took their meager possessions, ferried across the Ohio River, and settled near Pigeon Creek, close to what is now Gentryville, Indiana. Because it was winter, Thomas Lincoln immediately built a crude, three-sided shelter that served as home until he could build a log cabin. A fire at the open end of the shelter kept the family warm. At this time southern Indiana was a heavily forested wilderness. Lincoln described it as a "wild region, with many bears and other wild animals in the woods." [. . .]

Source #2: Loewen, James W. Lies My Teacher Told Me: Everything Your American History Textbook Got Wrong. New York: The New Press, 1995. 178.

The strange career of the log cabin in which Abraham Lincoln was born symbolizes in a way what textbooks have done to Lincoln. The actual cabin fell into disrepair probably before Lincoln became president. According to research by D. T. Pitcaithley, the new cabin, a hoax built in 1894, was leased to two amusement park owners, went to Coney Island, where it got commingled with the birthplace cabin of Jefferson Davis (another hoax) and was finally shrunk to fit inside a marble pantheon in Kentucky, where, reassembled, it still stands. The cabin also became a children's toy: Lincoln Logs, invented by Frank Lloyd Wright's son John in 1920, came with instructions on how to build both Lincoln's log cabin and Uncle Tom's cabin! The cabin still makes its archetypal appearance in our textbooks, signifying the rags to riches legend of Abraham Lincoln's upward mobility. No wonder one college student could only say of him, in a much-repeated blooper, "He was born in a log cabin which he built with his own hands."

1. The description the encyclopedia gives of Lincoln's childhood—the hard work, the honest poverty, and the succession of hand-hewn log cabins—is the story we are taught as school children.

2. James Loewen, in his book *Lies My Teacher Told Me*, focuses instead on the career of the log cabin Lincoln grew up in. He argues that the cabin's story symbolizes in some way what the textbooks students read have done to Lincoln (178).

3. It is interesting how the depiction of Lincoln's life in the *Encarta* encyclopedia is so focused on the domestic details. We can almost see the Lincoln family, huddled in the corner of their three-sided shelter, a small fire burning, as they wait for Father to build yet another log cabin.

4. According to Loewen, however, Lincoln's cabin has lead a comparatively unhealthy life. In his research he found that a new "Lincoln" cabin, a hoax built in 1894, was leased to two amusement park owners, went to Coney Island, where it got commingled with the birthplace cabin of Jefferson Davis. The cabin, shrunk down to fit inside a marble pantheon, now stands in Kentucky (178). Has the legend of Lincoln suffered the same fate?

Chapter 20

Writing the Research Project

EXERCISE 20-1 *Developing the Thesis*

Go back to the working thesis you developed in Exercise 16-2. After doing research on this topic for the exercises in Chapter 17, your thesis question, and perhaps even your topic and research questions, have most likely changed. Complete a new rubric to reflect these changes.

Topic:

Research question:

Working thesis:

EXERCISE 20-2 *Developing an Outline*

Using the advice given in Section 3d and in Chapter 20, develop an outline for your research paper (Exercise 20.1). Remember that your outline does not have to be a formal outline; use a system that works best for you.

EXERCISE 20-3 *Using Quotes, Summaries, and Paraphrases*

Below is a list of rhetorical situations. For each instance, decide whether you would quote, paraphrase, or summarize the sources mentioned. In some cases, you may want to do more than one.

1. You are writing an article arguing that a local judge is a racist. You have collected several inappropriate remarks made by this judge as she conducted the business of the court.
   (quote, paraphrase, or summarize)

2. You are writing an email to your mother comparing two recipes for chicken and dumplings you got from shows on the Food Network.
   (quote, paraphrase, or summarize)

3. You are trying to get the school computer lab you work at to buy some new multimedia software. Your supervisor hands you a stack of technical manuals and asks you to submit a proposal for the ones

you think the school should purchase. *(quote, paraphrase, or summarize)*

4. You are writing a paper on how Poe uses coded language in the poem "Annabel Lee" to criticize his deceased wife's family. *(quote, paraphrase, or summarize)*

5. You are writing a response to a letter in the newspaper. You want to emphasize the other author's lack of information about the subject. *(quote, paraphrase, or summarize)*

EXERCISE 20-4 *For Practice*

Following is a letter to the editor of a newspaper about a recent layoff at the largest technology firm in the city. Write a response to the letter (either positive or negative) in which you correctly incorporate a quote, a paraphrase, a summary, and a block quote.

October 13, 2002

To the editor,

I was laid off yesterday from my position as technical writer at TWMA.net. I had worked for TWMA.net for five years, had received stellar performance reviews, and had banked my future in the company's 401K. Imagine my surprise when I came in yesterday to a nearly empty building. It was nearly 10 A.M. and my supervisor, his supervisor, and even her supervisor could not be found. The few employees that were on my floor that day were milling about, wondering what was going on. At 10:15, over the loudspeaker, came the announcement. "TWMA.net regrets this decision, but due to the recent state of the market, TWMA.net has to make sacrifices. In order to keep the company viable, we have had to cut all of your jobs. We are sorry. Please leave your entry badge with the guard as you leave the building." Our computers were shut off at exactly 10:45. At 11:00, there were guards guiding us all to the doors. "It's not you... it's me," I could almost hear my ex-boyfriend saying. But we all know what he, and TWMA.net really meant with their hollow apologies: "so long, sucker!"

The past 24 hours, I've had nothing to do but worry and think. Here's what I've come up with so far—my proposed changes to the layoff process. (1) supervisors and executives have to be there to see the anguish on their employees faces as they get the axe. The guilt might be good for their souls. (2) No layoffs should be allowed until the company has made cuts in other areas, especially the company cars driven by the salespeople, executive travel, business lunches, extravagant gifts for clients, and upper management salaries. Only after the last salesperson has had to relinquish the keys to his or her Lexis SUV and the last CFO (Chief Financial Officer) has had to bring a sack lunch for the third week in a row can a regular employee be laid off. (3) Employees must be protected from their company's mismanagement of retirement funds. If an employee can not retrieve the funds they have worked so hard to save, someone in an Armani suit should go to jail.

As I left the building with my belongings (and whatever office supplies I could grab), I made a mental list of all the people who got to keep their jobs: the supervisors, the salespeople, the accountants, and those guys who work in Customer Service and spend all day gaming on-line. My job was sacrificed for theirs. TWMA.net has decided that they are worth more than I am.

I will openly admit that I am bitter. But I'm not the only one. And until the corporate world makes some changes, my brothers and sisters and I will be siphoning off unemployment like there's no tomorrow. 'Cause the way things are going, there just might not be.

Pounding the pavement,
Mary N. O'Connor

EXERCISE 21-1 *Using MLA-style In-text Citation*

Write a sentence or two incorporating the quotes provided using MLA-style in-text citation. Consider each source below to be one of several sources cited in the papers.

Quote: "Perhaps the most important problem in business management since the first industrial revolution began in Britain more than two centuries ago has been the coordination of manufacturing and marketing."

Author: Richard S. Tedlow
Source: *New and Improved*, p. xvii

_____

_____

_____

_____

_____

Quote: "How, then, is it possible to think new? How can new thoughts be crafted or cobbled out of material—words, sentences—itself 'pre-stressed' and irreparably secondhand (we think in words). How is any new philosophy conceivable when its only executive form is that of linguistic discourse, shuffling counters which have served already a billionfold?"

Author: George Steiner
Source: *Grammars of Creation*, p. 122

_____

_____

_____

_____

_____

EXERCISE 21-2 *For Practice: MLA List of Works Cited*

Select two books and at least one electronic resource for a paper you are planning to write. Then, create an MLA list of works cited by following the guidelines discussed in Chapter 21.

EXERCISE 21-3 *MLA-style Comparison*

Compare the MLA-style to the APA-style lists of works cited. (See Chapter 23 for more on the APA-style). What are the major differences between the two styles? What are the similarities? Hypothesize how and why these two standards for listing citations could have developed differently.

Chapter 22

Writing About Literature

EXERCISE 22-1 *Writing About Poetry*

Read the poem below by William Shakespeare. Then, write the rhyme scheme of the poem and scan the poem for its meter. Can you paraphrase the poem? What is lost in the process of paraphrasing the meaning of the poem?

My mistress' eyes are nothing like the sun;
Coral is far more red than her lips' red;
If snow be white, why then her breasts are dun;
If hairs be wires, black wires grow on her head.
I have seen roses damask'd, red and white,
But no such roses see I in her cheeks;
And in some perfumes is there more delight
Than in the breath that from my mistress reeks.
I love to hear her speak, yet well I know
That music hath a far more pleasing sound;
I grant I never saw a goddess go;
My mistress, when she walks, treads on the ground:
    And yet, by heaven, I think my love as rare
    As any she belied with false compare.

[Source: Shakespeare Online. 2000. http://www.shakespeare-online.com] (12/04/2002)]

EXERCISE 22-2 *Complex Arguments*

Read Sir Philip Sidney's sonnet [*Leave me, O love*] and ask yourself *what*, *how*, and *why* questions. Use the advice listed in section 22b to develop a complex argument about some action or idea in the poem.

[*Leave me, O love*]

Leave me, O love which reachest but to dust ;
And thou, my mind, aspire to higher things ;
Grow rich in that which never taketh rust,
Whatever fades but fading pleasure brings.
Draw in thy beams, and humble all thy might

To that sweet yoke where lasting freedoms be ;
Which breaks the clouds and opens forth the light,
That doth both shine and give us sight to see.
O take fast hold; let that light be thy guide
In this small course which birth draws out to death,
And think how evil becometh him to slide,
Who seeketh heav'n, and comes of heav'nly breath.

    Then farewell, world; thy uttermost I see;
    Eternal Love, maintain thy life in me.

[Source: *Poetry of the English Renaissance 1509-1660.* J. William Hebel and Hoyt H. Hudson, Eds. New York: F. S. Crofts & Co., 1941. 120.]

EXERCISE 23-1 *APA References*

Following APA conventions, create a reference section for a paper using the information provided below.

David Myers. *Psychology*. Holland, MI, Worth Publishers, 1998.

The Rites of Passage. Arnold Van Gennep. Translated by Monika B. Vizedom and Gabrielle L. Caffee. Published by The University of Chicago Press. London, England. 1960.

Marcel Mauss. 1990. *The Gift: The Form and Reason for Exchange in Archaic Societies*. Translated by W.D. Halls. W.W. Norton, publishers. New York City.

The Culture of Narcissism: American Life in An Age of Diminishing Expectations, by Christopher Lasch. Published in 1979 by W.W. Norton in New York City.

Money and the Morality of Exchange. Edited by J. Parry and M. Bloch in 1989 by Cambridge University Press in Cambridge, England.

EXERCISE 23-2 *For Practice: Online Treasure Hunt for APA Cites*

Using a search engine of your choice, perform an Internet search for online sources that use APA conventions when citing sources. Make a list of these Web sites and see if you can detect any common characteristics among the hosts of the Web sites. For example, do they all pertain to some aspect of psychology?

Chapter 24
CMS Documentation

EXERCISE 24-1 *CMS References*

Following CMS conventions, create a reference section for a paper using the information provided below.

George L. Mosse, *Nationalism and Sexuality: Middle Class Morality and Sexual Norms in Modern Europe*. Published in New York City by Howard Fertig in 1985.

Richard Boothby, *Death and Desire*. Published in New York City by Routledge Press in 1991.

Confidence Men and Painted Women: A Study in Middle-Class Culture in America, 1830-1870, by Karen Halttunen. Published by Yale University Press in New Haven, CT, in 1982.

Constructing Masculinity, edited by Maurice Berger, Brain Wallis, and Simon Watson (1995). Published by Routledge Press, New York City.

University of California Press, 1995. *Material Girls: Making Sense of Feminist Cultural Theory* by Suzanna Danuta Walters, published in London, England.

EXERCISE 24-2 *For Practice: Online Treasure Hunt for CMS Cites*

Using a search engine of your choice, perform an Internet search for online sources that use CMS conventions when citing sources. Make a list of these Web sites and see if you can detect any common characteristics among the hosts of the Web sites.

Chapter 25

CSE Documentation

EXERCISE 25-1 *CSE References*

Following CSE conventions, create a reference section for a paper using the information provided below.

> *Dictionary of Biology.* Indge, Bill. Dearborn Publishers, Dearborn, MI, 1999.

> David M. Raup's *Extinction: Bad Genes or Bad Luck*, published by W.W. Norton, 1992. New York City.

> *The Invisible Enemy: A Natural History of Viruses*, by Dorothy Crawford. London. Oxford University Press, 2000.

> K. Todd. New York City. (2001). *Tinkering With Eden: A Natural History of Exotics in America.* W.W. Norton.

EXERCISE 25-2 *CSE Conventional Comparisons*

Create a spreadsheet and compare the CMS, CSE, APA, and MLA conventions. What are the major differences between the four conventions? What are the similarities? Hypothesize how and why such different standards could have developed.

Chapter 26

Write with Power

EXERCISE 26-1 *Active Voice*

Underline the active or passive verb in the following paragraph. If a sentence contains a passive, rewrite the sentence to make it active.

Example:
    Many kinds of human behavior <u>are now being understood</u> as the products of brain structures by researchers in neuroscience.
Possible rewrite:
    Researchers in neuroscience now understand many kinds of human behavior as the products of brain structures.

It has been reported by researchers in neuroscience that food advertising often succeeds because of the structure of our brains. Some people are surprised by this finding. That people buy things they don't need because of advertising has long been rejected by economists. Studies using brain imaging have proven otherwise. When people see and smell their favorite food, a brain structure was found to be different from the neural circuits that are stimulated when we are truly hungry. When the dorsal striatum is activated, food is desired to be consumed, even if we are not hungry. Probably the dorsal striatum was important for human survival in past times when food wasn't plentiful. Food needed to be eaten and stored in our bodies for times when food wouldn't be available. But today with food everywhere, an epidemic of obesity is caused by the drive to eat when we aren't hungry.

EXERCISE 26-2 *Strong Verbs*

The paragraph below includes nouns used to express action. Underline all noun phrases that show action and the "be" verbs they follow. Then, rewrite the entire paragraph, changing the underlined nouns to verbs and deleting "be" verbs. More than one set of correct answers is possible.

Example:

may feel

An amputee <u>is likely to have the experience of</u> "phantom limb sensations," as the brain can misinterpret activity from the nervous system.

Possible Rewrite:

An amputee may feel "phantom limb sensations," as the brain can misinterpret activity from the nervous system.

Though few people celebrate the experience of pain, the human body is dependent on unpleasant impulses for survival. Without pain, an individual is at a disadvantage in terms of self-preservation. When a diseased brain is a failure at communication, the entire body is in jeopardy. Pain alerts the body to injured or strained joints, bones, or muscles and is integral in forcing an individual to alter his or her behavior to aid the healing process. Those who are without the ability to sense pain often die by early adulthood, as unchecked infections and injuries overwhelm the body.

[Source: Myers, David. *Psychology*. Holland, MI: Worth Publishers, 1998. 476-478.]

EXERCISE 26-3 *Living Agents*

In the paragraph below, underline the subjects of each sentence. Then, rewrite the entire paragraph so that living agents are performing the actions expressed by the verbs.

Example:

Historians have traced Halloween customs back to the time

<u>Halloween customs and traditions</u> have been traced back in
of the ancient Druids.

time to the ancient Druids.

The observation of these old customs in parts of Europe where the inhabitants are Celtic proves their Druid origin. To mark the beginning of winter, the burning of fires on November 1st was customary. These Halloween fires are lit even today in Scotland and Wales. Also, it was the belief of Druid custom that on the night of November 1st, the earth was roamed by such groups as witches, demons, and evil spirits. To greet the beginning of "their season," Halloween was the night when these demons celebrated the long nights and early sunsets of the coming winter. It was important to have fun at the expense of mortals on this night, and to offer treats as appeasement was the only way mortals could stop the evil, demonic tricks. To give these treats became a tradition, which has continued into modern Halloween celebrations.

[Source: Welser, Francis X.. Christian Feasts and Customs. New York: Harcourt, Brace and Co., 1952. (315).]

EXERCISE 27-1 *Rewriting the Wordy Passages*

The paragraph below is littered with redundant words and phrases. Rewrite wordy sentences to make them more concise.

Example:
> Threatening in concept, black holes are often incorrectly thought of as an astronomical force that possesses a pull so strong in force it can engulf anything in its path.

Possible Rewrite:
> Black holes are often incorrectly thought of as threatening, an astronomical force that possesses a pull so strong it can engulf anything in its path.

Because we cannot visibly see a black hole up-close distance-wise, we must use our own imaginations to consider its characteristic properties. For example, imagine taking a jumping leap feet first into a black hole. As you fell, you would descend downward at a slow speed; however, from your personal perception you would seem to be falling faster in speed as time elapsed. In fact, a personal friend observing your downward descent would see that you were in fact moving more and more slowly. In addition, that self-same friend would see that your body was being elongated lengthwise as the center of the black hole pulled more strongly in force on the part of your body which was closest in distance to its center. Simultaneously, your body would begin to start collapsing toward its center, as the forceful force pulled both sides of your body toward the middle of the black hole's center. Unlike in science fiction make-believe, black holes do not serve as either a menacing threat to human life or as a possible means of space or time travel.

[Source: Seeds, Michael A. *Foundations of Astronomy*. Belmont, CA: Wadsworth Publishing Company, 1992. 313-314.]

EXERCISE 27-2 *Empty Intensifiers*

In the paragraph below, underline empty intensifiers and the modifiers they intensify. Replace these with more specific and effective modifiers.

Example:

an extensive

The American CIA conducted a ~~very long~~ search for a drug that could serve as a truth serum.

In 1942, the American Office of Strategic Services (OSS) Chief William Donovan gathered six incredibly respected scientists to develop a truth serum. The American Psychiatric Association and the Federal Bureau of Narcotics, both very respectable organizations, also participated in this rather secretive search for the truth drug. After definitely varying results and very interesting visions occurred with drugs such as peyote and scopolamine, the group turned to marijuana as a really serious possibility. Creating very different forms of the drug, both strong and diluted, the group tested knowing and unknowing subjects. They tried incredibly unique methods of administering the drug such as placing a laced gel in foods or injecting a serum into cigars or cigarettes, but they found it very hard to settle on an exact dosage or suitable method. Also, they discovered that individuals did not react very regularly, and the drug could cause a subject to become either absolutely too talkative or particularly quiet. Despite the initial setbacks with marijuana, the American government would really pursue its quest to find a really good substance to serve as a truth serum.

[Source: Lee, Martin A. and Bruce Shlain. *Acid Dreams - The Complete Social History of LSD: The CIA, the Sixties, and Beyond*. New York: Grove Press, 1992. 3-5.]

EXERCISE 27-3 *Eliminate Wordiness*

The paragraph below includes many unnecessary and wordy phrases. Rewrite each sentence to eliminate wordiness. Make sure you retain the original meaning of each sentence.

Example:
    Due to the fact that at this point in time historians dispute the origin of the necktie, I will not make an attempt to provide one conclusive answer.
Possible rewrite:
    Because historians now dispute the origin of the necktie, I will not try to provide one conclusive answer.

In the modern world today, it seems the necktie is considered one of the oldest fashion creations and one of the earliest items created for the sole purpose of decorating the human form. One of the main theories locates the predecessor of the modern necktie in the neighborhood of the mid-sixteen hundreds when Croatian soldiers arrived in France adorned with tasseled scarves of linen and muslin. It was at this point in time when the French dubbed these types of garments "croates," which soon became "cravats." In a very real sense, this garment with regard to social practice developed a significance for the purpose of determining levels of proper masculinity; as a matter of fact, at one point in time, the ability to properly tie a necktie served as an initiation ritual for marriage or military service. In spite of the fact that the emphasis placed on tie tying has waned, some historians use this association of proper masculinity with the practice of tie tying in order to explain the short life of the clip-on tie.

[Source: Lehnert, Gertrud. *A History of Fashion In the 20th Century.* Cologne, Germany: KönemannVerlagsgesellschaft mbH, 2000. 70-71.]

EXERCISE 27-4 *Rewriting for Clarity and Concision*

The following paragraph includes negative constructions and both properly and improperly placed expletives (*there is, there are, it is,* etc.). Rewrite the sentences for clarity and concision.

Example:
   Not unlike anthropology and sociology, paleontology attempts to uncover information that is yet unknown about both living things and civilizations.
Possible rewrite:
   Similar to anthropology and sociology, the discipline of paleontology attempts to uncover new information about both living things and civilizations.

   There are a number of ways fossils can help paleontologists gain additional information about ancient eras. Though not without problems and informational gaps, fossils aid in locating data that is missing regarding location, time, and traits of both past and future organisms. For example, data has been determined by the not uncontested notion of "uniformitarianism," a theory that assumes certain interactions of matter have not been inconsistent throughout time. Because there is this assumption regarding the constancy of certain processes, it is not illogical to believe there is a way by which fossil age and other characteristics may be determined by considering the effects of constant processes on the aged relic. There is controversy in the scientific community, however, regarding the constancy of such scientific processes and interactions.

[Sources: Simpson, George Gaylord and William S. Beck. *Life: An Introduction to Biology*. New York, Chicago, and Burlingame: Harcourt, Brace & World, Inc., 1965. 756-757.
Newman, William L. *Geologic Time – Online Edition.* <http://www.uta.edu/geology/geol1425earth_system/1425chap6.htm>]

Chapter 28

Write with Emphasis

EXERCISE 28-1 *Combining Sentences for Emphasis*

The following paragraph includes many short sentences. Locate the main and subordinate ideas, and combine groups of sentences into longer, more concise, and clearer sentences. In the revised sentences, underline the main information twice and the subordinate information once.

Example:

Muscular Christianity was popular in the late nineteenth and early twentieth centuries. It sought to change the image of Jesus Christ.

Possible rewrite:

Popular in the late nineteenth and early twentieth centuries, Muscular Christianity sought to regain the church for men by changing the image of Jesus Christ.

American religion was thought of as a very feminine in the nineteenth century. It catered to moralism. Some thought it deterred market capitalism. There were more women than men in congregations. Pictures of Jesus Christ portrayed a sickly, effeminate man. Men wanted to reclaim religion. They did not want to aspire to an effeminate God. They wanted to change the image of Jesus. They refocused on Jesus' carpentry. Carpentry was associated with America's self-made man. Billy Sunday was a major spokesman for Muscular Christianity. He was an ex-professional baseball player. He had left baseball. He disapproved of the fact that one did not need morality for success in baseball. He demanded men be manly like Jesus. He was popular. *American Magazine* voted him the eighth greatest man in the United States. This vote was in 1914. This helped to rejuvenate religion. Men were allowed to be religious. They were also allowed to be strong.

[Source: Kimmel, Michael. *Manhood in America: A Cultural History.* New York: The Free Press, 1996. 175-181.]

EXERCISE 28-2 *Practice with Parallelism*

The paragraph below contains many examples of nonparallel sentence structure. Underline the faulty constructions and either delete them or replace them with parallel constructions, as necessary.

Example:
 Sesame Street introduced America to educational children's
     provided
 television and providing children with informational

 furry friends.

  Sesame Street entered the American consciousness in 1969,

playing, singing, and to teach. Joan Ganz Cooney, a major mastermind

of *Sesame Street*, proposed to join child-friendly techniques with

commercial television standards, and accelerating the speed of teaching.

These standards and techniques would aid teachers' goals of teaching

symbolic representation, cognitive processes, and teaching social and

physical environments. These goals were accomplished with the help of

live actors, using puppeteers, and animation. In its more than thirty year

run, *Sesame Street* has managed to educate three generations of school

children, finding a home in over 140 countries, and garner more Emmys

than any other show in history.

[Source: Borgenicht, David. *Sesame Street Unpaved.* New York: Children's Television Workshop, 1998. 14-17.]

EXERCISE 28-3 *Revising for Parallelism*

You're invited to Howard's party on Saturday. The following directions to Howard's house contain several examples of faulty parallelism. Revise the directions, making the structure of each parallel to the first entry.

Directions to Howard's
 1. Turn left onto Route 22 N at the end of Maple Street.

2. You'll come to the Dewdrop Inn after following Route 22 N 3 miles.
3. There's a sharp right turn onto Geoffrey Drive at the fourth traffic signal after the Dewdrop.
4. The red mailbox you're looking for is halfway down the block.
5. Directly across from the mailbox there's a driveway—turn in there.

You can reverse the directions and follow them to come home.

Chapter 29
Find the Right Words

EXERCISE 29-1 *Writing in Standard American English*

The following paragraph from a research paper contains slang that may not be appropriate for its audience, a Women's Studies professor. Revise the paragraph to make all the sentences edited American English.

Example:

> most famous
> Sally Ride is ~~super famous~~ as the first American
> woman in space and as the youngest astronaut to orbit in the
> *Challenger* Shuttle.

In her youth, Ride was a radical tennis player. However, instead of becoming a professional athlete, she went to Stanford and received her doctorate in x-ray physics. While at Stanford, Ride was selected out of a group of 8,000 other folks to be part of NASA's astronaut class. On June 18, 1983, Ride took her totally extreme first trip to space. In 1989, Ride split NASA and became a professor of physics at USSD, where she directs the California Space Institute. Ride was so awesome in space that she totally had an impact on women in scientific and technical careers.

[Source: Welch, Rosanne. Encyclopedia of Women in Aviation and Space. Santa Barbara: ABC & CLIO, 1998. p. 188-9.]

EXERCISE 29-2 *Formal or Informal?*

Sue Mills wrote the following note to thank her friend Hannah Le Chat for dinner. How would the language of the note change if Sue Mills were writing a letter to a potential employer, thanking her for a luncheon interview? Rewrite the note, making the potential employer the audience. Note how eliminating colloquialisms changes a letter's level of formality.

Dear Hannah,

I'm so glad that we were finally able to catch up on things at lunch on Friday. I thought the eggplant was totally off the hook, the beans were to die for, and the cheesecake melted in my mouth. All in all, you totally raised the roof with that one. Even if my back were against the wall, I would still be a fish out of water in the kitchen. As a matter of fact, ever since my junior high cooking teacher bawled me out in front of the class, I've really had a chip on my shoulder about my culinary skills. Anyway, I just wanted to give you props for the lunch and let you know I hope we can strap on the old feedbag again sometime soon.

Well, I should *beat it.*

Sue

EXERCISE 29-3 *Eliminating Colloquial Language*

The following paragraph is taken from a rough draft of a research paper for an Environmental Ecology class. The instructor asked the writer to eliminate any use of first person, colloquial language, unnecessarily big words, and wordiness. Use the advice from this section to revise the paragraph according to the instructor's comments.

Example:

> Many geologists and conservationists in the United States have views that are diametrically opposed on whether to support or fight mining and commercialization in sacrosanct public acreage.

Possible rewrite:

> Many U.S. geologists and conservationists disagree on whether to mine or commercialize public lands.

David Brower, who died in 2000, was a person who was the President of the American wilderness preservation club called the Sierra Club. As this organization's preeminent leader he was the human personification of preservation. Brower took a no-holds-barred approach to fighting the infidels of mining and tourism in America's wilderness areas. I think his most perspicacious campaign against these factors that threaten the wilderness must have been when he published an ad to fight the commercialization of the Grand Canyon. His placement of newspaper advertisements telling people about plans to open businesses at the base of the canyon deterred this development. I think that most who believe in conservation would agree that these achievements make David Brower a hero for the American environment.

[Source: Coyle, Daniel. "The High Cost of Being David Brower." Outside Online, December 1995.
<http://www.outsidemag.com/magazine/1295/12f_high.html>]

EXERCISE 29-4 *Connotations*

The following sets have similar denotative meanings but differ in connotation. Put a plus (+) over words that have positive connotations and a minus (-) over words that have negative connotations. Put an equal sign (=) over words that are neutral in connotation. If you are unsure of the meaning of a word, use a dictionary.

1. thin, skinny, gaunt, slender, sleek, lean, emaciated, bony, skeletal, slight, lanky

2. music, cacophony, noise, tune, song, discord, racket, harmony, clamor

3. hard worker, drudge, diligent, nose to the grindstone, workaholic, industrious, plodder, assiduous, painstaking, drone, thorough

Jon Antonioni's political science professor asks his students to write a brief self-evaluation about each paper they write. The following passage is Jon's self-evaluation of his paper arguing that the United States should not renew most-favored-nation status for China. Jon knows he did not do his best work on the paper, and he wants to be honest about that but avoid hurting his ethos as a student who cares about the class. As practice in using words with the right connotations, revise his evaluation to (1) strengthen his ethos without bending the truth and (2) offer evidence to back up his assertions.

Jon Antonioni
Politics in the United States
Self-assessment

This is my worst paper of the semester. After beginning my research at 11 the night before it was due, I realized I was in deep trouble. I was stupid to assume the issue of MFN status could be mastered in a few hours. However, I did my best, cramming in as much research as I could before I started writing. Because it was so late, I decided to skip writing a boring outline. But when I started cranking out the draft, the thesis started to seem ridiculous a few paragraphs in. I got confused about where the thesis was headed. Instead of going back to the beginning, though, I kept churning out pages. The result was that I had a different argument at the beginning than I did at the end. With the little time I had left, I squeezed in as much revising as I could to try to make the thesis consistent throughout. I think the argument I ended up with would have worked all right, had I not chosen to play video games all week instead of starting my paper.

EXERCISE 29-6 *Using Specific Language*

This paragraph, from a research paper about space exploration, contains vague and incorrect language. Revise it to eliminate vague language, misused homonyms, and misused sound-alike words. Information you may need to eliminate vague language is included in parentheses.

Example:
　　Astronauts have been exploiting space for quite a few years now.
Possible rewrite:
　　Astronauts have been exploring space since at least the 1960s.

Space missions can adversely affect an astronaut's health. A more than minor culprit is the lack of gravity in space; one of the affects that weightlessness has on astronauts is that it causes bone loss, which might be really bad. A sort-of older (45) astronaut may have such serious bone deterioration that after a mission, her bones resemble those of an old lady (like an 80-year-old). Other continuous effects are the interruption of sleeping patterns and the deterioration of the immune system and mussels. But perhaps the scariest affect sited by experts is radiation exposure, especially during visits to Mars. None knows what the cancer risks from this exposure might be.

EXERCISE 29-7 *Selecting the Right Word*

Underline the correct word in parentheses in the following paragraph. Look up the words in a dictionary if you are not sure of their meaning.

Butchering a hog requires (patience, patients) and hard work. First, find a (cite, sight, site) outside (wear, where) you will have plenty of space. After killing the pig, dunk it in hot water to loosen the (coarse, course) hair. Scrape the hair with a knife (continually, continuously) until the skin is completely (bare, bear). Thread a gambling stick (threw, through) the hamstrings, and hang the pig head-down from a post. Remove the head, cut down the length of the spine and remove the tenderloin, fatback, ribs, middlin' meat, shoulders, and hams (respectfully, respectively). While some people are squemish about eating hogs' heads and organs, in (principal, principle) nearly every part of the animal is edible.

EXERCISE 29-8 *Figuring Out Figurative Phrasing*

Using the types of figurative language stated in parentheses, invent sentences that convey the ideas represented in the following paragraph.

Example:

The 1956 explosion of Bezymianny, a Russian volcano, was shocking to area residents since the volcano was assume to be dormant. (simile)

Possible rewrite:

The 1956 explosion of Bezymianny, a Russian volcano, came like the return of Lazarus to area residents; the volcano was assumed to be dormant.

After the 1956 explosion, Bezymianny's ash covered everything around it; days later, the ash had even reached Alaska and Britain. (metaphor) Trees fifteen miles away were knocked down by the explosion. (metaphor) The same as Mount St. Helens, the Bezymianny eruption began with a large avalanche and then exploded sideways. (metonymy) Since its 1956 eruption, Bezymianny has erupted every so often, causing its neighbors to fear the volcano in their midst. (synecdoche)

EXERCISE 29-9 *Overusing Clichés*

The paragraph that follows is filled to the brim with clichés. Underline each cliché and replace with fresh language.

Example:

Cephalopods are a group of marine mollusks that many
find distasteful
Americans would not touch with a ten-foot pole.

However in Japan and in the Mediterranean, squid, octopus, and cuttlefish are an important food source and sell like hotcakes. Unfortunately, myths about giant squid sinking boats and octopus drowning swimmers persist in the United States, and information that giant squid are weak as kittens and that an octopus has never drowned anyone falls on deaf ears. The Japanese attitude is a step in the right direction; they see the octopus as a cheerful, friendly creature and often use its image as a toy or mascot. Our culinary pleasures could grow by leaps and bounds if more of us opened our minds to the joys of fried calamari dipped in marinara sauce and squid sushi with plenty of wasabi. We need to wake up and smell the coffee in the United States that cephalopods are under-exploited marine resource.

[Source: Davidson, Alan. *The Oxford Companion to Food.* Oxford University Press.]

Chapter 30

Write to be Inclusive

EXERCISE 30-1 *Eliminating Stereotypes*

The following paragraph includes numerous assertions based on stereotypes, both positive and negative. Rewrite the sentences to eliminate the stereotypes. More than one correct answer may be possible.

Example:
> Surly, artistic, and foreign, New Yorkers exemplify the American melting pot.

Possible rewrite:
> With their diverse cultural heritage, New Yorkers exemplify what is considered the American melting pot.

Throughout the borough of Manhattan in New York City, widely diverse groups live and work together. Manhattan's single women brazenly forgo family lives for careers, high-powered suits, and Park Avenue apartments, while gays and literary types make an artistic home in Greenwich Village. Modern-day geishas and samurais abound in North America's largest Chinatown, where visitors can find an Asian feast most any time of day. A jazzy dance north brings one to Harlem, famous for the Apollo Theater, where one can see African Americans display their musical abilities, and Sylvia's Soul Food, a restaurant rivaled only by its greasy-spoon counterparts in the Deep South. New York City is the perfect place for a wide-eyed Texan or Midwesterner to escape the cultural sameness of their home regions and experience a true American city.

[Source: <http://www.visitnyc.com> 15 Aug 2001.]

EXERCISE 30-2 *Using Inclusive Language: Gender and Sexual Orientation*

The following paragraph includes instances where writing is not inclusive with regard to gender and sexual orientation. Rewrite the sentences to be more inclusive.

Example:
  Controversy followed the 1993 "Don't Ask, Don't Tell" policy which altered the ban on homosexuals in the military.
Possible Rewrite:
  Controversy followed the 1993 "Don't Ask, Don't Tell" policy which altered the ban on gay men, lesbians, and bisexuals in the military.

Fulfilling his campaign promise, President Clinton pursued the annihilation of the military policy that limited the enlistment of servicemen based on sexual preference. In 1993 a compromise called "Don't Ask, Don't Tell" went into effect, thereby permitting the enlistment of any soldier as long as he avoided any public disclosure of his sexual orientation. Because of the semantics of the policy, effeminate men and masculine girls are still under threat of witch-hunts and discharges. Under the current policy, if a soldier has revealed his homosexuality to anyone (including a parent, clergyman, or psychologist), he can be discharged. Though "Don't Ask, Don't Tell" arose out of an attempt to alleviate bias toward gays in the military, the boys and girls in Congress merely reconfigured the presence of bias in the armed forces.

[Source: *Servicemembers Legal Defense Network.* <http://www.sldn.org/templates/get/record.html?record=23> 15 Aug 2001.]

EXERCISE 30-3 *Using Inclusive Language: Race/Ethnicity*

The following paragraph includes instances where the writing is not inclusive with regard to race, ethnicity, and other differences. Underline these words or phrases and replace with better alternatives.

Example:

the diverse ethnic and socioeconomic groups

American census data examines <u>both poor, uneducated blacks</u> living in the United States. and <u>rich Orientals</u>.

Various organizations gather census data in order to observe patterns of growth or decline in many areas of American life. By identifying where old people live, for example, questions regarding politics, special interests, and marketing can be answered. Florida has one of the highest and Utah one of the lowest percentages of people over the age of sixty-five. By identifying this pattern, marketers can target the elderly. Statistics regarding employment of the old are also found to intersect with those regarding handicapped people, since old people are usually also handicapped. A recent poll showed that the dumb and lame had less than a 25% employment rate. Based on the data provided, it would not be unwise to guess that these unfortunates also live in Florida. Furthermore, nobody speaks English in south Florida.

[Source: <http://www.ameristat.org> 15 Aug 2001. <http://www.census.gov> 15 Aug 2001.]

78

Chapter 31

Write for Diverse Audiences

EXERCISE 31-1 *Understand English as a Global Language*

Interview two or three classmates whose language backgrounds are different from your own. For example, you may interview a speaker of a different variety of English and a native speaker of Korean. Ask each to describe his or her relationship with the English language—when, where, and how they learned English, what variety of English they use, what language they speak at home, at work, when they travel to different countries, and how they choose which language to speak when their audience can speak more than two languages.

EXERCISE 31-2 *Respect Differences in Language and Culture*

Identify your pet peeves in writing. Do you have any words or phrases that you find unnecessary, annoying or wrong? Write down as many of them as possible. Then, consider where and how your acquired the negative attitude toward them. Bring the list of your pet peeves and the sources of your attitude. Then, discuss with your classmates when those words and phrases may be useful or appropriate.

Chapter 32

Grammar Basics

EXERCISE 32-1 *Sentence Patterns*

Classify each of the following sentences in three categories. First, is it declarative, interrogative, imperative, or exclamatory? Second, is it positive or negative? And third, is it passive or active?

Example:

America boasts some of the world's strangest museums, from the American Sanitary Plumbing Museum to the Museum of Questionable Medical Devices. *declarative, positive, active*

1. Don't miss the Spam memorabilia display in Austin, Minnesota's First Century Museum. _____

2. The Combat Cockroach Hall of Fame in Plano, Texas displays a roach dressed like Marilyn Monroe!_____

3. Does the Elvis Is Alive Museum in Wright City, Missouri really have a Tomb Room? _____

4. Stand in the mouth of a four-and-a-half story high fiberglass muskie at the National Fresh Water Fishing Hall of Fame in Hayward, Wisconsin. _____

5. The Desert of Maine Museum was not built in a desert at all, but in snowy Freeport, Maine. _____

[Source: Gurvis, Sandra. *America's Strangest Museums: A Traveler's Guide.* Syracuse, N.J.: Citadel Press 1996.]

EXERCISE 32-2 *Functions of Nouns*

The underlined words in the paragraph below are nouns. Identify the function of each of the nouns. Do they serve as subjects, objects, subject complements, objects of a preposition, or modifiers of another noun?

Example:

Subject   object of preposition

The original <u>title</u> for *Casablanca* was
subject complement
Everybody Comes to Rick's.

The boyish <u>Ronald Reagan</u> was the studio's first <u>choice</u> for the male <u>lead</u>. Instead, the <u>studio</u> chose <u>Humphrey Bogart</u>, the shrapnel-scarred tough <u>guy</u>, to portray the <u>owner</u> of <u>Rick's</u> <u>nightclub</u>. The Swedish <u>actress</u> <u>Ingrid Bergman</u> was eventually cast as the female <u>lead</u>. The unexpected <u>chemistry</u> between <u>Bergman</u> and <u>Bogart</u> made *Casablanca* one of the greatest <u>films</u> of all <u>time</u>.

[Source: Turner Publishing, Inc. <u>Casablanca: As Time Goes By</u>. Atlanta, GA.: Turner Publishing, 1992. p. 49, 50, 64.]

EXERCISE 32-3 *Functions of Pronouns*

The underlined words in the paragraph below are pronouns. Identify the function of each. Do they serve as personal, possessive, demonstrative, indefinite, relative, interrogative, reflexive, or reciprocal pronouns?

Example:

On November 20, 1820, a sperm whale rammed and sank the
Possesive pronoun
whaleship *Essex*, but all the sailors escaped with <u>their</u> lives.

The ramming was no accident; after the whale hit the *Essex* once, <u>it</u> turned around to hit the ship a second time. The sailors found <u>themselves</u> adrift in three whaleboats, 1,200 miles from the nearest islands. However, the crew feared that <u>those</u> islands were populated by cannibals. After a month starving at sea, the sailors found a small island, <u>which</u> offered little to eat. Crushed by hunger, the crew convinced <u>each</u> <u>other</u> to eat a fellow sailor who had died of starvation. <u>Who</u> could say that <u>anybody</u> would act differently if placed in similar circumstances? <u>Their</u> chances of survival weakened with each passing day. Yet, first mate Owen Chase navigated <u>his</u> whaleship for eighty-eight days until the crew was rescued by a merchant ship.

[Source: Philbrick, Nathaniel. *In the Heart of the Sea.* New York: Viking, 2000.]

EXERCISE 32-4 *Functions of Verbs*

Underline the verbs in the following paragraph. Decide whether the verb is a main verb or an auxiliary verb. If it is an auxiliary verb, note if it is a modal verb or not.

Example:

> aux not modal/main
>
> Frank Oz <u>has</u> <u>created</u> some of the   best known characters on *Sesame Street,* including Bert, Cookie Monster, and Grover.

Frank Oz was born in Hereford, England, in 1944 and began staging puppet shows when he was 12. You may know him best as the voice of Yoda in the *Star Wars* series. Oz could have remained a puppeteer, but he has decided to embark on a second career as a movie director. You might have seen one of his movies such as *Indian in the Closet* or *In and Out.* The Muppet Fozzie Bear is named after Oz, using his first initial and his last name.

EXERCISE 32-5 *Verbals*

Underline the verbals in the following paragraph and identify whether they are infinitives, participles, or gerunds. In addition, specify whether the participle verbals are past or present participles.

Example:

> Gerund   past participle
>
> <u>Casting</u> the "evil eye" is a superstition <u>recognized</u> in cultures around the world.

The evil eye is a focused gaze, supposedly causing death and destruction. Writings of the Assyrians, Babylonians, Greeks, and Romans all document an abiding belief in this supernatural concept. Old women and those thought to be witches are often accused of having the evil eye. To ward off the effects of the evil eye, people have resorted to praying, hand gestures, and purifying rituals.

[Source: Gifford, Jr., Edward S. "Evil Eye." *Collier's Encyclopedia.* 1996.]

EXERCISE 32-6 *Modifiers*

The underlined words in the following paragraph are modifiers. Label each modifier adjective or adverb and state which word it modifies.

Example:

    adverb/living   adjective/woman
    After <u>initially</u> living the life of an <u>average</u>
adjective/woman   adverb/became
    <u>middle-class</u> woman, Dorothy Parker <u>ultimately</u> became
      adverb/infamous adjective/wits
    one of the <u>most</u> <u>infamous</u> wits of the
adjective/century
    <u>twentieth</u> century.

Parker's father encouraged her to pursue "<u>feminine</u> arts" such as piano and poetry, but <u>just</u> following his death in 1913, she rushed into what turned out to be a <u>profitable</u> foray into the world of literature. <u>Almost</u> <u>immediately</u>, Vanity Fair purchased one of her poems, leading her into a <u>full-time</u> <u>writing</u> position with Vogue. It was <u>life-changing</u>, as Parker's flair for <u>clever</u> prose <u>swiftly</u> led her into the inner sanctum of New York <u>literary</u> society. Parker was fired from Vanity Fair's editorial board in 1919 after <u>harshly</u> panning an advertiser's film. Despite her <u>early</u> departure from magazines, Parker gained <u>lasting</u> fame as a <u>prolific</u> writer and critic.

[Source: MacGill, Frank. *Great Lives From History: American Women Series.* Volume 4. Pasedena and Englewood Cliffs: Salem Press, 1995. 1404-1407.]

EXERCISE 32-7 *Prepositional Phrases*

Underline the prepositional phrases in the paragraph below and circle the prepositions.

Example:

During the 1964 presidential campaign, Lyndon B. Johnson waged a dynamic campaign against Barry Goldwater with great success.

Johnson's campaign, inspired by the New Deal of Franklin Roosevelt's administration, was attractive to members of both political parties. According to Johnson's idea of the "Great Society," America would eliminate prejudice, poverty, and other social ills. In addition to the support of Democrats and social liberals, Johnson received approval from a large portion of the American media, which had traditionally lauded Republican candidates.

[Source: Gifford Jr., Edward S. "Democratic Party." *Collier's Encyclopedia.* New York: Collier's, 1996. 91.]

EXERCISE 32-8 *Subordinate and Coordinate Conjunctions*

Fill in the blank with an appropriate coordinate or subordinate conjunction. More than one conjunction may fit.

Example:

Scientists used to believe that sharks attacked people intentionally, _*but*_ they now assert that sharks attack humans only when mistaking them for natural prey.

Only four of the 400 species of shark attack humans: bull sharks, whitetips, tiger sharks, _____ great whites. _____ sharks committed 74 fatal attacks in the past 100 years, 75% of all shark attack victims have survived. Peter Benchley, the author of *Jaws*, describes sharks as "fragile" _____ their numbers seem to be declining.

_____ the populations of some shark species have declined by 80%, some nations have enacted laws to protect them. People are coming to see sharks as an important part of ocean environments, _____ they are acting accordingly.

[Source: Benchley, Peter. "Great White Sharks." National Geographic. April 2000.]

EXERCISE 32-9 *Identifying Word Classes*

Each underlined word in this paragraph represents one of the word classes explained in this section. Identify nouns, pronouns, verbs, verbals, adjectives, adverbs, prepositions, conjunctions, articles, and interjections.

Example:

Preposition   adjective

After the horrific space shuttle Challenger disaster in 1986,

Pronoun   noun

everyone hoped America would never have to see such

a tragedy in the space program.

On a clear Texas morning in February of 2003, onlookers waited patiently to observe the reentry and landing of the space shuttle Columbia. They were hoping to witness a bit of history, but   no one had any way of knowing just how historic or heartbreaking that day would be. While cruising over Texas, the hurtling shuttle transformed into a ball of flame. Boom! The sounds of explosions rang out as the as the tragically doomed shuttle shed debris over Texas, Arkansas, and Louisiana. Families and dignitaries waited at Florida's Kennedy Space Center, unaware of the tragedy that had occurred. Soon thereafter, the American president would heartily reaffirm the United States' commitment to the future of the space program.

[Source: *Newsweek*, Feb 10, 2003 p22 "Out of the Blue" by Evan Thomas.]

EXERCISE 32-10 *Clause Patterns*

Identify which of the three main clause patterns each sentence below exemplifies: subject-verb-object, subject-verb, or subject-linking verb.

Example:

In 1954, the United States Supreme Court ordered school desegregation. subject-verb-object

1. Arkansas Governor Faubus refused the order.
   _____

2. The Arkansas militia seemed impenetrable.
   _____

3. Nine African-American students retreated from the school.
   _____

4. Eisenhower ordered National Guard troops to escort the African-American students.
   _____

5. The guardsmen were successful.
   _____

[Source: Taylor, AJP and JM Roberts. *Purnell's History of the 20th Century.* Volume 9. New York and London: Purnell, 1974. 2289-2290.]

EXERCISE 32-11 *Kinds of Clauses*

The subordinate clauses in the sentences below are underlined. Identify whether they are noun, adjective, or adverb clauses.

Example:

adverb clause
Although many cultures abhor the practice of cannibalism,
noun clause
that it has taken place in many areas is indisputable.

1. Tribes in the West Indies who sought dominance over neighboring peoples often ate human flesh.

2. Some practitioners in New Guinea and West Africa believed that consuming the body of an enemy would transfer the special attributes of the conquered to themselves.

3. It is important to note that not all tribes <u>who practiced human sacrifice</u> necessarily condoned consumption of the dead.

4. <u>Unless there were dire circumstances of famine</u> most tribes perceived cannibalism solely as a byproduct of military conquest.

5. <u>That cannibalism is a purely non-Western phenomenon is a common misconception; because Mediterranean histories cite instances of cannibalism</u>, we must concede that it has had a long and diverse cultural existence.

[Source: Halsey W.D., Friedman E. "Cannibalism." *Collier's Encyclopedia.* 1984. 350, 351.]

EXERCISE 32-12 *Identify the Phrases*

Identify the underlined phrases in the following sentences. Are they prepositional, verbal, appositive, or absolute phrases? If they are verbal phrases, specify whether they are infinitive phrases, participial phrases, or gerund phrases.

Example:

participial phrase
<u>Reaching peak capacity between 1892 and 1924</u>, Ellis Island
prepositional phrase
was the initial point of contact <u>for countless new American immigrants.</u>

1. <u>Arriving on Ellis Island,</u> immigrants <u>seeking American citizenship</u> were herded <u>into long lines for medical inspection.</u>

2. <u>Surviving this process</u> enhanced one's chance <u>to remain here.</u>

3. <u>To check immigrants' eyelids</u> for diseases was a procedure examiners commonly performed <u>with non-medical objects, including hairpins and buttonhooks.</u>

4. Trachoma, an eye disease, was often diagnosed <u>in immigrants,</u> and resulted <u>in their deportation.</u>

5. Judgments <u>of the immigrants' mental stability</u> also affected entry status, <u>decisions often seeming highly subjective.</u>

[Source: *Ellis Island Official Website.* <http://ellisisland.com> 12 Jul 2001.]

EXERCISE 32-13 *Clauses*

In each of the sentences below, underline the main clause. If there are subordinate clauses, underline these twice. Then identify what type of sentence each sentence is: simple, compound, complex, or compound-complex.

Example:

<u><u>Although many cultures consider death an ending or something to fear,</u></u> <u>various Meso-American civilizations see it as something to embrace,</u> and <u>it is this belief</u> <u><u>that gives rise to the celebration known as The Day of theDead.</u></u> *compound-complex*

1. The dead reappear during the month-long celebration.

   _____

2. The goddess Mictecaclhuati presides over all the festivities, but each culture celebrates the festival in its own unique way.

   _____

3. Some revelers celebrate by eating candy skulls with the names of their deceased relatives written on the foreheads.

   _____

4. In some parts of Mexico, family members picnic at the spots where the deceased have been buried. _____

5. Because Spaniards found the ritual blasphemous, they moved it to coincide with the Christian holiday All Saints' Day, but their attempt to destroy it failed since the celebration still thrives today.

_____

[Source: "Indigenous People Would Not Let Day of the Dead Die." <http://www.azcentral.com/rep/dead/history/> 12 Jul 1901.]

EXERCISE 32-14 *Complex Sentences*

The following are simple sentences. Rewrite each as compound, complex, and compound-complex sentences.

Example:

Simple: Baseball, America's national pastime, has endured war, scandal, and players' strikes.

Compound: Baseball has endured war, scandal, and players' strikes, yet it is still America's national pastime.

Complex: Baseball, which many consider America's national pastime, has endured war, scandal, and players' strikes.

Compound-

Complex: While it remains America's national pastime, baseball has endured many trials, and none were more traumatic than war, scandal, and players' strikes.

1. Philip K. Wrigley, chewing-gum entrepreneur, founded the All-American Girls Professional Baseball League in 1943, bolstering waning interest in baseball during the onset of American involvement in World War II.

    Compound:

    _____

    _____

Complex:

_____

_____

Compound-Complex:

_____

_____

2. The league attracted women from all over the United States and Canada, providing them with a previously absent national venue to showcase their athletic talents.
   Compound:

   _____

   _____

   Complex:

   _____

   _____

   Compound-Complex:

   _____

   _____

3. The league peaked in 1948 with ten teams and over 900,000 paying fans.
   Compound:

   _____

   _____

   Complex:

   _____

   _____

Compound-Complex:

_____

_____

4. Promoting an image of femininity among female athletes, the league
   insisted on strict regulations regarding dress and public behavior.
       Compound:

   _____

   _____

       Complex:

   _____

   _____

       Compound-Complex:

   _____

   _____

5. Lacking audience interest, the league folded in 1954.
       Compound:

   _____

   _____

       Complex:

   _____

   _____

       Compound-Complex:

   _____

   _____

[Source: All-American Girls Pro Baseball League Official Website
<http://www.aagpbl.org> 13 Jul 2001.]

Chapter 33

Fragments, Run-ons, and Comma Splices

EXERCISE 33-1 *Sentence Fragments*

Each of the following passages contains a fragment. Revise to eliminate the fragment.

Examples:

Certain mammals, like flying squirrels and sugar gliders, are
varieties that actually ~~glide. Which~~ glide, which enables them to survive when hunted by nimble predators.

1. Flying squirrels, like typical squirrels except they have flaps of skin that allow them to glide.

2. Flying squirrels glide gracefully. From tree to tree with surprising ease.

3. To gain speed and momentum, flying squirrels often free-fall for several feet. Then to turn in midair, lower one arm.

4. The Japanese giant flying squirrel is one of the largest known varieties. Spanning two feet long from its head to its furry tail.

5. By gliding, escape predators and gather food quickly.

[Source: Kernan, Michael. "How Squirrels Fly." *Smithsonian*. 31:11 (February 2001) 32-36.]

EXERCISE 33-2 *Revising to Eliminate Fragments*

Find the fragments in the following paragraph and revise the paragraph to eliminate them.

Barton Springs still seems like a place not in Texas for those who come from elsewhere. Surrounding hills covered by live oaks and mountain juniper. And ground around the pool shaded by pecan trees whose trunks are a dozen feet in circumference. Banana trees and other tropical plants grow in the roofless dressing areas of the pool. With grackles whistling jungle-like sounds outside. The pool is in a natural limestone creek bed. Which is an eighth of a mile long. Fed by 27,000,000 gallons of 68° water bubbling out of the Edwards Aquifer each day.

EXERCISE 33-3 *Run-on Sentences*

The following are run-on sentences. Correct each one following the steps given in Chapter 33.

Example:

> Japanese Kabuki theater surfaced in the early 1600s its [1600s. Its] origins are often linked to the public, improvised performances of Izumo Grand.
>
> Japanese Kabuki theater surfaced in the early 1600s. Its origins are often linked to the public, improvised performances of Izumo Grand.

1. The original Kabuki troupes were mostly comprised of female dancers however male performers replaced them after the art became associated with prostitution.

   _____

   _____

2. Performances included several thematically linked elements such as dance, history, and domestic drama they lasted up to twelve hours.

   _____

   _____

3. In the 1700s, choreographers and special schools became commonplace and Kabuki dance became more complex.

   _____

   _____

4. Kabuki costumes are often quite elaborate actors sometimes need assistance preparing for performances.

   _____

   _____

5. Since World War II, Western influences have altered the social position of Kabuki ticket prices have risen, making performances more accessible to tourists, but not the average Japanese citizen.

_____

_____

[Source: Brockett, Oscar. *History of the Theatre*. Needham Heights: Simon and Schuster, Inc., 1991. 266-271.]

EXERCISE 33-4 *Comma Splices*

The following sentences all contain comma splices. Eliminate the splices using the methods indicated in the parentheses.

Example:

Accused Nazi propagandist Leni Riefenstahl was born in Germany in 1902, her films Triumph of the Will and Olympia are said to have captured the essence of the Nazi era. (split into two sentences)

Accused Nazi propagandist Leni Riefenstahl was born in Germany in 1902. Her films *Triumph of the Will* and *Olympia* are said to have captured the essence of the Nazi era.

1. Riefenstahl spent her early days performing in Germany as a dancer, a 1924 knee injury derailed her dance career, detouring her into a successful, scandal-ridden life in film. [split into two sentences, add a conjunctive adverb]

_____

_____

2. Early editing work prepared her to direct her first film, *The Blue Light*, however, national recognition was slow to come. [add a semicolon]

_____

_____

3. The year 1935 saw the release of Riefenstahl's film *Triumph of the Will*, which stunningly captured a Nazi Party rally, to be sure, this film forever cast a shadow over the director's career. [split into two sentences]

_____

_____

4. Her documentary of the 1936 Berlin Olympics, *Olympia*, captured the spirit of athletics, her pioneering techniques such as the underwater camera solidified her place in film history. [convert one clause to a participial phrase]

---

5. Her films were deemed Nazi propaganda, the French imprisoned Riefenstahl, her film career was forever damaged by insinuations, despite the eventual ruling that she was not an active member of the Nazi Party. [make into a compound-complex sentence]

[Source: Acker, Ally. *Reel Women: Pioneers of the Cinema 1896 to the Present.* New York: The Continuum Publishing Company, 1991. 298-303.]

Chapter 34
Subject-Verb Agreement

EXERCISE 34-1 *Verb Tense Review*

Write the correct present tense form of the verb in the sentences below.

Example:
   Suzi <u>writes</u> in her journal everyday. (write)

1.   Aaron _____ the piano. (play)

2.   The sisters _____ their mother. (resemble)

3.   I_____ a new DVD player. (want)

4.   He _____ for days without taking a bath. (go)

5.   You _____ me laugh. (make)

EXERCISE 34-2 *Singular and Plural Subjects*

In the sentences below, underline the subject and decide whether it should be treated as singular or plural. Next, circle the verb. If the verb doesn't agree in number with the subject, revise it to agree.

Example:
   Various <u>regions</u> in Italy—including Tuscany, Lazio, and
   possess
   Umbria—⟨possesses⟩ rich cultures that center around food

preparation and meals.

1. Some cite Rome's Marcus Gavius Apicius as the author of the first
    cookbook, written in the first century.

2. Each Italian city and town in Italy possess a historical rationale for
    the gastronomical traditions of today.

3. People in central Italy enjoy eating many types of meat, but neither beef nor liver outshine the popularity of the region's top meat, pork.

4. Cheese, as well as foods such as balsamic vinegar and olive oil, is sometimes named for the region where it is produced.

5. Almost every man and woman in America know spaghetti hails from Italy, but many fail to learn the rich and varied Italian tradition of food.

[Source: Plotkin, Fred. *Italy Today: The Beautiful Cookbook.* New York: Harper Collins Publishers, 1997. 133-137.]

EXERCISE 34-3 *"One of Those" Exercises*

Each sentence below uses a "one of those...who" construction. Underline the subject and circle the verb. Correct the verb if it does not agree in number with the subject.

Example:
Babe Didrikson ☐aharias is only one of those great female
are
athletes who (is) lost to younger generations, often

overshadowed by the splashy television images of athletes of

the second half of the twentieth century.

1. Born in south Texas in 1911 and overcome with a passion for sports, Didrikson ☐aharias was not one of those girls who was wiling away the hours dreaming of wearing dresses, catching boys, and settling down.

2. Because she qualified for five events for the 1932 Olympics, Didrikson ☐aharias was only one of those women who was affected by the regulation prohibiting female athletes from competing in more than three Olympic contests.

3. The United States Golf Association president was only one of those officials who banned Didrikson □aharias from tournaments in order to prevent her from overwhelming the competition.

4. In addition to excelling in basketball, tennis, bowling, baseball, and track and field and winning three Olympic gold medals, Didrikson □aharias was one of those athletes who was responsible for creating the Ladies Professional Golf Association.

5. Didrikson □aharias stands as only one of those women who defy the notion that girls cannot swing, throw, or run; yet her early death from cancer stands as a stark reminder of the frailty of even the most impressive human form.

[Source: Schwartz, Larry. "Didrikson Was a Woman Ahead of Her Time." *E S P N . c o m .* 9 Jul 1998. <http://espn.go.com/sportscentury/features/00014147.html>.]

EXERCISE 34-4 *Indefinite Pronouns*

The indefinite pronouns in each of the following sentences have been underlined. Write down whether each indefinite pronoun is singular or plural. Then, circle the verb and correct it if it does not agree in number with the subject.

Example:

Because stand-up comedy has traditionally been a male
                          SINGULAR   has
dominated industry, <u>each</u> successful female comics (have)

struggled against the grain.

1. Of those who overcame the gender barrier, <u>few</u> are more beloved than Lily Tomlin, the creator of Ernestine, the telephone operator, and Edith Ann, the precocious child in the jumbo rocking chair.

2. <u>Each</u> of her characters were introduced to the American public when she burst onto the scene in the 1960s and 1970s on shows such as *Laugh-In, Sesame Street,* and *Saturday Night Live.*

3. <u>Most</u> of Tomlin's films in the 1980s—including *9 to 5, All of Me,* and *The Incredible Shrinking Woman*—were greeted with mixed reviews.

4. <u>Neither</u> Tomlin's cultural critiques nor her sketch comedy were wholeheartedly embraced by the networks.

5. <u>Each</u> of the many female comics of today owe homage to women like Lily Tomlin, Phyllis Diller, and Joan Rivers for paving the way.

[Source: Martin, Linda and Kerry Segrave. *Women in Comedy.* Secaucus: Citadel Press, 1986. 366-379.]

EXERCISE 34-5 *Collective Nouns*

The following sentences contain collective nouns that can be considered either singular or plural depending on the context. Underline the correct form of the verb that agrees with the subject.

Example:
> The jury (<u>is</u>/are) ready to deliberate. [*jury* is considered singular] The jury (<u>believe</u>/believes) that they will resolve their differences in judgment. [*jury* is considered plural]

The administration usually (try/tries) to avoid responsibility for issues concerning students living off campus, but also (listen/listens) when the city government (complain/complains) about student behavior. The public (is/are) upset about large parties that last into the morning. The university formed a committee of students, faculty, and neighborhood residents to investigate the problem. Unfortunately, the committee (disagree/disagrees) about the causes of excessive noise.

EXERCISE 34-6 *Tricky Subjects*

Each of these sentences contains a tricky subject. Write down whether the underlined subject is singular or plural. Circle the verb and correct the verb if it does not agree in number with the subject.

Example:
Despite the racist overtones of nineteenth-century minstrel
shows, the <u>United States</u> ~~have~~ *(has)* a rich tradition of African

American theater dating back to the 1820s.

1. African-American <u>theatrics</u> dates back to 1821, the year John Brown organized the first troupe of African-American actors.

2. Despite the controversy connected to Brown's involvement in the Harper's Ferry riots, <u>thanks</u> is due to him for creating a space where African Americans could publicly perform works such as *Richard III* and *Othello*.

3. Because American <u>politics</u> was incongruous with supporting serious African-American art, the troupe's lead actor, Ira Aldridge, moved to London.

4. <u>Politics</u>, not talent or ambition, was a driving force in determining the success of non-Anglo performers for decades.

5. Despite the success of twentieth-century actors such as Sydney Poitier, James Earl Jones, and Alfre Woodard, nearly <u>one hundred thirty years</u> are a long time for African American actors to wait for popular acceptance.

[Source: Brockett, Oscar. *History of the Theatre*. Needham Heights: Simon and Schuster, 1991. 421-422.]

EXERCISE 35-1 *Verb Forms*

Underline the verbs in the following paragraph and write the verb form for each. You may find some forms more than once. Choose from the following:

base form
-sl-es form
past tense
past participle-past perfect
past participle-passive
past participle-adjective
present participle-present perfect
present participle-gerund
present participle-adjective

Example:

Animal baiting, (*present participle-gerund*) a gruesome predecessor to dueling (*present participle-adjective*) cocks, found (*past*) great success in the medieval era.

Recent lobbying efforts by animal rights groups are illustrating how drastically contemporary beliefs regarding animal safety differ from beliefs in medieval times. History shows that the torturing of taunted animals such as bears and bulls was considered a sport in medieval times. At bullbaitings, organizers tethered a bull to a pivot point in the middle of an arena and unleashed a snarling dog that taunted the bull. Once the bull ceased to amuse the crowd, he found himself on the quick route to the nearest butcher shop.

EXERCISE 35-2 *Irregular Verbs*

Underline the correct form of the irregular verb in the following paragraph.

Example:

I Love Lucy, (thinked/<u>thought</u>) of by many as that funny show with the zany redhead, (<u>drove</u>/drived) many television innovations.

After marrying in 1940, Lucille Ball and Desi Arnaz (strived/strove) to create their own television situation comedy. However, the networks feared audiences would not accept a Cuban leading man married to an Anglo woman and (sought/seeked) to block their project. Thus, Ball and Arnaz decided to fund the show independently, and within a short time the couple (got/gotten) together the money, created Desilu Studios, and (began/begun) shooting their pilot. Soon Amreicans (eated/ate), (drunk/drank), and (slept/sleeped) *I Love Lucy*. With innovations like the three-camera technique, Desilu Studios (laid/lain/layed) the groundwork for future sitcoms and (rode/ride/rided) into television history.

EXERCISE 35-3 *Transitive and Intransitive Verbs*

In the following sentences decide whether the sentence calls for a transitive or intransitive verb and underline the correct choice.

Example:

The eastern diamondback rattlesnake (will set/<u>will sit</u>) immobile for hours, sometimes coiled and sometimes stretched to its full length of seven feet.

A rattlesnake will often (lay/lie) in wait for its favorite meal: a rat. When encountering one of these poisonous snakes, (set/sit) aside your assumptions about aggressive snakes; many are timid. You can tell a rattlesnake feels threatened if his tail (rises/raises) and you hear a sharp rattling sound. If you are hiking in the desert of the southwestern U.S., do not (sit/set) down without carefully surveying the ground. To (rise/raise) your chances of avoiding a rattlesnake bite, make noise when you are hiking in wilderness areas.

[Source: Bahr, L.S.; Bloomfield, L.A.; Johnston, B. "Rattlesnake." *Collier's Encyclopedia*. 1996. 672.]

EXERCISE 35-4 *Verb Tense Review*

Read the entire paragraph and then underline the correct verb tenses in the parenthesis.

Example:

The American Indian Movement (AIM) (<u>originated</u>/ originates) in Minneapolis in 1968.

Native-American activists, including Dennis Banks and Russell Means, (created/ create) AIM, a militant organization to fight for civil rights for American Indians. AIM members (participate/ participated) in a number of famous protests, including the occupation of Alcatraz Island (1969-1971) and the takeover of Wounded Knee (1973). The group (has helped/ helps) Indians displaced by Government programs, (will work/ has worked) for economic independence for Native Americans, and (agitates/ has agitated) for the return of lands (seize/ seized) by the U.S. government. In his book, *Agents of Repression: The FBI's Secret War Against the Black Panther Party and the American Indian Movement*, Ward Churchill (documented/ documents) how the FBI (infiltrated/ infiltrates) AIM in an attempt to destroy it. While most local chapters of AIM (have disbanded/ disbands), Native-Americans activists today still (fight/ fought) for their autonomy and for compensation for centuries of oppression and economic injustice.

[Source: "The American Indian Movement." *Encyclopedia Britannia.* Volume 1. 331-332.]

EXERCISE 35-5 *Indicating Mood*

In the sentences below, identify the mood of the underlined verbs: indicative, imperative, or subjunctive.

Example:

When elected in 1960, John Fitzgerald Kennedy <u>became</u> (indicative) the nation's youngest and first Roman Catholic president.

Using the slogan "Let's <u>get</u> (　　　　　) this country moving again," Kennedy <u>fought</u> (　　　　　) against unemployment and a sluggish economy. His insistence that U.S. technology <u>be</u> (　　) on par with that of the Soviets <u>contributed</u> (　　　　　) to his popularity. In his inaugural speech, he <u>expressed</u> (　　　　　) his desire that Americans "<u>bear</u> (　　　　　) the burden of a long twilight struggle . . . against the common enemies of man: tyranny, poverty, disease, and war itself." His desire that all citizens <u>regard</u> (   ) themselves as participants in a growing democracy is evident in his famous words, "<u>Ask</u>

(   ) not what your country can do for you—ask what you can do for your country."

[Source: "John Fitzgerald Kennedy." *Encyclopedia Britannica*, Vol. 6, 1998. 799.]

EXERCISE 35-6 *Subjunctive Forms*

Underline the correct subjunctive form of the verb in each sentence below.

Example:

> If you (are/<u>were</u>) to go more than 100 feet below water during a deep sea dive, you might experience what is commonly called "rapture of the deep."

Rapture of the deep results when nitrogen levels elevate in the bloodstream because of added pressure, and the diver begins to feel as if she (was/were) invincible. Often the combination of nitrogen and excessive oxygen overwhelms the diver, causing her to wish that she could (gets/get) free of the breathing apparatus. If a diver (was/were) above the surface of the water, she would experience one atmosphere of pressure. At 100 feet below, however, the pressure is tripled. It is crucial that a diver (prepare/prepares) for the possibility of rapture occurring. To get used to this disorienting sensation, some divers inhale nitrous oxide to see how they would handle themselves if they (are/were) in the throes of rapture of the deep.

[Source: "Nitrous in Diving"
www.resort.com/~banshee/Info/N2O/nitrous.diving.html]

Chapter 36

Pronouns

EXERCISE 36-1 *Picky about Pronouns*

Underline the pronoun in each sentence of the following paragraph and replace the pronoun if it is incorrect.

Example:

The American Dietetic Association (ADA) offers several tips

|

on snacking for <u>you</u> and ~~me~~ to learn.

   If you and a friend go on a road trip, the ADA suggests that you and her limit your stops at fast food restaurants. The association suggests us snacking in the afternoon provided we choose foods that are healthy for you and I. If your friend wants a cheeseburger for lunch you should respond that you and her could split the meal. For your sake and me, it is not a good idea to snack after dark.

[Source: www.eatright.org/healthy/snacking.html "Snacking" American Dietetic Association.]

EXERCISE 36-2 *Whose Pronoun is it Anyway?*

In the sentences below, fill in the blank with the correct pronoun: who, whom, whoever, whomever.

Example:

Soon the Japanese people will select new additions to Parliament, some of <u>whom</u> are prominent celebrities.

1. Seats in Japanese Parliament have lately gone to candidates _____ have high ambitions, fame, and no political experience.

2. Atsushi Onita is a professional wrestler _____ cries "Fire!" when he enters the ring and _____ believes in parental supervision of children.

3. One of the candidates for _____ many will vote is Emi Watanabe, a former Olympic figure skater _____ deplores the mounting costs of health care.

4. _____ the Japanese vote for, one thing is certain.

5. _____ wins will have done so after an unprecedented wave of sports star campaigning.

[Source: French, Howard W. "Japanese Parties Hope Celebrities Will be a Ticket to Success." *New York Times*. 29 Jul 2001.]

EXERCISE 36-3 *Pronoun Review*

The sentences below include all the pronoun situations explained in this section. Underline the correct pronoun in each sentence.

Example:
(<u>We</u>/Us) scholars generally look at subjects from a critical distance, but we must never forget to impose that critical distance on our own lives too.

1. The gurkhas are a division in the British armed forces (who/whom) originate from Nepal.

2. Between 1814 and 1816 several Nepalese hill tribes successfully contained the advancing British army, even though the British were far more technically advanced than (they/them) were.

3. Thinking that, "(Us/We) warriors should stick together," the British enlisted the Nepalese tribesmen to fight in the specially formed gurkha division.

4. (Whomever/Whoever) wished to join the gurkhas had to know someone already serving in the British army; it was an extremely prestigious battalion to be a part of.

5. (Its/It's) amazing to think that nearly 200 years later, money earned from gurkha pensions and salaries constitutes the largest single source of foreign exchange for the Nepalese economy.

[Source: Cowley, Robert and Geoffrey Parker. *Military History*. Boston: Houghton Mifflin. 195-96.]

EXERCISE 36-4 *Determining the Antecedent*

In the following sentences, pronouns are separated from the nouns they replace. Underline one antecedent and fill in the pronoun that agrees with it in the blank provided.

Example:
> Ironically, <u>greyhounds</u> are rarely gray; <u>their</u> fur can be all shades of red, brown, gray, and brindle.

1. Canine experts disagree on the origin of the name "Greyhound", but may believe _____ derives from "Greek Hound."

2. For over 5,000 years, greyhounds have been prized for _____ regal bearing and grace.

3. English Greyhounds were introduced into England by the Cretans around 500 BC, but _____ are most famous for being mascots for America's number one bus line.

4. King Cob was the first notable greyhound sire recorded after England began documenting canine pedigrees in 1858, and _____ fathered 111 greyhounds in three years.

5. Each greyhound King Cob fathered was of the purest pedigree, even though _____ great-grandfather was a bulldog.

[Source: Halsey, William D. and Emanuel Friedman. "Greyhound," "Greyhound Racing." *Colliers Encyclopedia.* New York: Macmillan, 1984. 452-3.]

EXERCISE 36-5 *Pronoun Review II*

Underline the indefinite pronouns, collective nouns, and compound antecedents in the paragraph that follows. Circle the related pronouns, and, if necessary, revise them to agree with their antecedents. In some cases, you have to decide if the emphasis is on the group or individuals within the group.

Example:
> Almost <u>everyone</u> can remember the first time (he or she) saw
>
> *The Sound of Music*, the story of the <u>ex-nun</u> and (her) Austrian
>
> <u>family</u> who use (their) ingenuity to escape the Nazi Anchluss.

Neither the three films nor the stage play used their time to tell the complete and accurate story of the real Maria von Trapp; however, the audience often believe(s) what they see(s). Americans associate Maria with their pixie-ish icon, Julie Andrews, but few would recognize the real Maria if he saw her. As in the American musical, Maria, Captain von Trapp, and the children fled her home. The real family did use its singing skills to evade the Nazis during a concert, but afterward, it settled in a lodge in Stowe, Vermont. Everyone who visits the lodge finds themselves surrounded by a bit of cultural history.

[Source: Trapp Family Lodge Website. http://trappfamily.com/history.html. 16 Jul 2001.]

EXERCISE 36-6 *Pronouns and Gender Bias*

The following sentences contain examples of gender bias. Identify where the gender bias problem lies, and rewrite the sentences using subject/pronoun formations that are unbiased. See if you can avoid using "his or her" constructions.

Example:

> When an American turns eighteen, he is bombarded with advertisements that market the easy allure of credit.
>
> When Americans turn eighteen, they are bombarded with advertisements that market the easy allure of credit.

1. When someone is financially overextended, he often considers credit cards as a way of making ends meet.

2. One might begin to convince himself that credit is the only way out.

3. But each adult must weigh the advantages and disadvantages of her own credit card use.

4. Eventually, one may find himself deep in debt because of high credit rates and overspending.

5. Then, one option might be for the individual to find a debt consolidator to assist him.

[Source: Manning, Robert D. Credit Card Nation: The Consequences of America's Addiction to Credit. New York: Basic Books, 2000.]

Chapter 37

Modifiers

Exercise 37-1 *Comparatives and Superlatives*

Decide whether each word in parentheses should be comparative or superlative. Rewrite each word adding either the correct suffix (-er or –est) or more or most. If you find an absolute modifier (a word that should not be modified), underline it.

Example:

most popular

With over 23 million models sold since 1966, the (popular) car in the world is the Toyota Corolla.

1. The (good) selling car in the United States is the Toyota Camry, closely followed by the Honda Accord and the Ford Taurus.

2. At 41,907 the U.S. has the (high) number of road deaths per year; however the (bad) motor vehicle accident occurred in Afghanistan in 1982, when 300 people died after an oil tanker exploded in a tunnel.

3. If you are traveling a long distance, a car might not be the (convenient) form of transportation.

4. A train can travel at speeds exceeding 160 miles per hour, but if you want something (rapid) the U.S. military's X-15 aircraft travels an (impossible) 4,520 miles per hour!

5. London's Heathrow, the world's (busy) airport, serves over 48 million travelers per year.

[Source: Ash, Russell. *The Top Ten of Everything*: 2000. New York: DK Publishing, 1999. 230, 232-233, 235, 239-241.]

Exercise 37-2 *Double Negatives*

Revise the following paragraph to eliminate any double negatives. More than one answer may be correct in each case.

Examples

      can

One can't hardly survey the history the American film industry without encountering the story of the "Hollywood Ten," one of the main groups of artists targeted as Communists.

After the creation of the House Un-American Activities Committee (HUAC), Cold War paranoia could not barely hide itself in post-World War II America. HUAC followed on the coattails of the 1938 Special Committee on Un-American Activities. This earlier committee did not focus not solely on Communists; extremists from both the far left and the far right were targeted. By the 1940s, however, HUAC focused not on neither white supremacist nor pro-Nazi groups, but instead on the supposed Communist infiltration of Hollywood. Scarcely no one could escape the grasp of HUAC; actors, producers, and directors all came under scrutiny. By the end of the proceedings, not hardly nobody remained unscathed. Hundreds in the entertainment industry were either fired or appeared on the infamous HUAC blacklist.

[Source: "The 1947 HUAC Hearings and The Hollywood 10." The Hollywood 10 Website. <http://www.hollywood10.com> 16 Jul 2001.]

EXERCISE 37-3 *Tricky Adjective / Adverb Pairs*

The words in parentheses below are tricky adjective/adverb pairs. Underline the word(s) being modified in the sentence, and underline the correct adjective or adverb from the pair.

Example:

To ensure successful space travel, NASA has tackled the challenge of enabling astronauts to eat (healthy/healthfully) in space so that they can stay (good/well).

111

In the early days of manned space missions, NASA had (fewer/less) problems feeding astronauts. But the (further/farther) astronauts traveled, the (further/farther) NASA had to go to ensure healthy eating in space. For example, the Mercury missions of the early 1960s took (fewer/less) time than an actual meal, so NASA's (real/really) challenge didn't come until crews were in space for longer periods of time. However, these shorter trips worked (good/well) as testing sites for experimental astronaut foods. By the mid-sixties, those on the Gemini missions were offered better ways to prepare and enjoy foods in space. Engineers eventually discovered that packaging foods in an edible liquid or gelatin would prevent them from crumbling and damaging the equipment (bad/badly). By the Space Shuttle expeditions of the eighties and nineties, (real/really) headway had been made in terms of (good/well) dining technology, and crew members could devise their own menus rather than rely on (bad/badly) prepared dinner-in-a-tube.

[Source: NASA Website.
<http://spacelink.nasa.gov/Instructional.Materials/Curriculum.Support/Life.Scie nce/Living.and.Working.in.Space/Space.Food.and.Nutrition> 23 Jul 2001.]

EXERCISE 37-4 *Ambiguous Phrases and Clauses*

Underline the adjective phrases and clauses in the following paragraph. If any phrases or clauses could apply to two subjects, revise the sentence to eliminate ambiguity.

Example:

> Arriving June 19, 1865, the Texas slaves were informed of their freedom by Union soldiers two years after the signing of the Emancipation Proclamation.
>
> Arriving June 19, 1865, the Union soldiers who informed Texas slaves of their freedom came two years after the signing of the Emancipation Proclamation.

1. Now known as Juneteenth, Texas celebrates the day Texan slaves discovered their freedom.

2. A release from daily pressures, freed slaves celebrated annually their day of emancipation.

3. Celebrated vigorously in the fifties and sixties, the Civil Rights movement sparked a renewed interest in the Juneteenth holiday.

4. Still going strong, entertainment, education, and self-improvement are all activities included in the annual celebration.

[Source: Official Juneteenth Website. <http://www.juneteenth.com> 17 Jul 2001.]

EXERCISE 37-5 *Ambiguous Adjectives*

Underline the one-word adjectives in the following paragraph. If any are placed ambiguously or incorrectly, revise them.

Example:

first female

The incomparable Loretta Lynn was the <u>female first</u> singer to be inducted into the Songwriters Hall of Fame.

Lynn rose from a Kentucky sheltered childhood to earn the title "First Lady of Country Music," garnering awards various and honors. At the young age of fourteen, a pregnant Lynn felt lost as she joined her husband Doolittle in Washington state, but their both lives would change when he bought Lynn her first guitar. Country music lovers were receptive to prolific Lynn's lyrics and tales of female strength. Maintaining a music successful career, Lynn has continued to write and perform these all years.

[Source: Official Loretta Lynn Website. <http://lorettalynn.com/bio.htm> 16 Jul 2001.]

EXERCISE 37-6 *Squinting Modifiers*

Rewrite each of the following sentences, moving the adverb in order to eliminate squinting modifiers. Place adverbs where they make the most logical sense within the context of the sentence. Underline the adverbs in your revised sentences.

Example:

In the mid-1800s, Father Gregor Mendel developed experiments ingeniously examining the area of heredity.

In the mid-1800s, Father Gregor Mendel ingeniously developed experiments examining the area of heredity.

1. Mendel's work focused on initially hybridizing the Lathyrus, or sweet pea.

2. The Lathyrus possessed variations conveniently composed of differing sizes and colors.

3. Hybridizing the plants easily allowed Mendel to view the mathematical effects of dominant and recessive trait mixing.

4. By crossing white-flowered pea pods with red-flowered pea pods, Mendel proved successfully existing pairs of hereditary factors determined the color characteristics of offspring.

5. Though published in 1866, Mendel's theory of heredity remained unnoticed mostly by the biological community until the early 1900s.

[Source: Simpson, George Gaylord and William S. Beck. *Life: An Introduction to Biology*. New York, Chicago, and Burlingame: Harcourt, Brace & World, Inc., 1965. 166-169.]

EXERCISE 37-7 *Descriptive Modifiers*

Underline the disruptive modifiers in the following paragraph. You may find a modifying clause or phrase that separates major components of a sentence, or you may find a split infinitive. Then, rewrite the paragraph to eliminate the disruptions. More than one way of revising may be correct.

Example:

The Catholic papacy, <u>because of conflict in the Papal States</u>, resided in France for more than seventy years.

Because of conflict in the Papal States, the Catholic papacy resided in France for more than seventy years.

In the thirteenth and fourteenth centuries, the Italian Papal States, because of militantly rivaling families, were consumed in chaos. In 1305 the cardinals elected, unable to agree on an Italian, a Frenchman as the new Pope. He decided to temporarily remain in France. The papacy would, because of various religious and political reasons, remain in France until 1378. Rome, during the papacy's seventy-year absence, would lose both prestige and income.

[Source: "Brief History of the Avignon Papacy." <http://www.chat.carleton.ca/~damstutz/history.htm> 17 Jul 2001.]

Exercise 37-8 *Dangling Modifiers*

Each sentence below contains a dangling modifier. Revise the sentences to eliminate dangling modifiers according to the methods named in section 37e. More than one way of revising may be correct.

Example:
> Though it preceded Woodstock, popular music history often obscures the Monterey Pop Festival.
>
> Though the Monterey Pop Festival preceded Woodstock, it is often obscured by popular music history.

1. Lasting for three days in June of 1967, over thirty artists performed.

2. The largest American music festival of its time, attendance totaled over 200,000.

3. With artists such as Ravi Shankar, Otis Redding, and The Who, the fans encountered various musical genres.

4. Performing live for the first time in America, fans howled as Jimi Hendrix set his guitar on fire.

5. Establishing a standard for future festivals, Woodstock and Live Aid would eventually follow suit.

[Source: "Monterey." <http://www.visi.com/~astanley/rad/monterey.html> 19 Jul 2001. "The Way to Monterey." <http://www.stg.brown.edu/~ed/monterey.html> 19 Jul 2001.]

Chapter 38

Commas

EXERCISE 38-1 *Comma Review*

Underline conjunctive adverbs, introductory phrases, and long introductory modifiers in the following sentences. Then set off those elements with commas when necessary.

Example:

Although king cobras have small fangs, one bite is poisonous enough to kill an elephant.

1. King cobras in fact have a poisonous bite from the moment they are born.
2. Even though king cobras carry lethal venom women in Thailand's King Cobra Club dance with the snakes' heads in their mouths.
3. Also many Southeast Asian countries worship the king cobra.
4. Above all avoid provoking king cobras; they are not aggressive animals if left undisturbed.
5. An antidote is available however if you are bitten by a cobra.

EXERCISE 38-2 *Commas and Coordinating Conjunctions*

Decide which of the coordinating conjunctions in the following sentences should be preceded by commas and add them.

1. The band Abba was only together from 1974 to 1982 yet their hit "Dancing Queen" is still popular today.
2. Abba is best know for their music but they also made a movie entitled *Abba, The Movie.*
3. The quartet's two married couples had success as musicians but not as husbands and wives.
4. After their divorces, group members parted ways and began solo careers.
5. Abba's songs no longer top the charts but in 2001 their music was featured in a Broadway musical called *Mamma Mia.*

[Source: liner notes. *Abba Gold.*]

EXERCISE 38-3 *Modifiers and Commas*

The underlined portions of the paragraph below are modifiers. Identify each as either a restrictive or nonrestrictive modifier. Then, set off the nonrestrictive modifiers with commas.

Trajan decided to use the Empire's coffers <u>which were brimming with war booty</u> to begin a massive building program. He commissioned the market <u>Mercati Traianei</u> and a lush new forum. In AD 113 he also built a column <u>still on display in Rome today</u>, adorned with reliefs depicting his military victories. But the conditions <u>that many Romans faced day to day</u> stood in stark contrast to the splendor Trajan created. <u>Living in cramped apartment buildings</u> people coped with dark, dirty, and sometimes cold homes.

EXERCISE 38-4 *Series and Commas*

Insert commas to separate items in a series. Place a check in front of any sentence that does not require commas.

Example:
　　　Suburban residents unknowingly spread diseases among deer by
　　　feeding them salt, corn, and pellets.

1.　White-tailed deer ground squirrels gray squirrels foxes raccoons coyotes opossums and armadillos are often in my back yard.

2.　White-tailed deer and coyotes are among the animals that have adapted best to urban habitats.

3.　Deer find cover in urban green belts and thrive on young trees, shrubs,and flowers that homeowners plant.

4.　White-tailed deer reproduce quickly because they have always been prey animals for wolves, coyotes mountain lions bobcats and bears.

5.　Elimination of predators, curtailment of hunting and a high birth rate have led to deer overpopulation in many urban areas.

EXERCISE 38-5 *Adjective Series and Commas*

Identify each underlined adjective series below as either coordinate or cumulative. Then insert commas to separate coordinate adjectives.

While an <u>average meat-eating</u> American eats approximately 70 pounds of pork per year, China leads the world in pork consumption. Prior to 1900 pork was the most popular meat in the United States; however today, the <u>other white</u> meat is less widely eaten than beef. Since no part of the pig goes unused and it can be easily preserved, pork is an <u>economical versatile</u> meat. In addition, the <u>wily resourceful</u> pig can forage for food when its owner cannot provide for it. It seems likely that meat eaters across the globe will continue to enjoy <u>various pork</u> products, like bacon, ham, and sausage, daily.

EXERCISE 38-6 *Comma Review*

Proofread the paragraph below for errors using commas with quotations. Some are used correctly. Cross out unnecessary commas, move misplaced commas, and add omitted commas.

Craquelure is, "the fine network of cracks that scores the surface of paintings." (Elkins 20) Elkins explains that "few museum visitors realize how many paintings have been seriously damaged" and goes on to list possible hazards, such as damage by, "fire, water, vandalism, or just the wear and tear of the centuries." (20) Not all cracks are signs of legitimate age; indeed "Counterfeiters have faked cracks by putting paintings in ovens, and they have even rubbed ink in the cracks to make them look old." (Elkins 22) Though cracks often happen with mishandling, Elkins explains that, "most cracks in paintings that are not caused by accidents are due to the flexing of the canvas or the slow warping of the wood." (22) If you are serious about art history, you may want to learn how to read the cracks in art work. "*Craquelure* is not a hard-and-fast method of classifying paintings," admits Elkins "but it comes close." (24)

EXERCISE 38-7 *More on Commas*

The fictional business letter that follows has omitted commas with dates, numbers, personal titles, place names, direct addresses, and brief interjections. Insert commas where they are needed.

Mazaces' Headquarters
Cairo Egypt

13 December 332 BC

Parmenio
Commander of Syria
Damascus Syria

Dear Parmenio:

Thank you for your latest correspondence Parmenio dated December 9 332 BC. I am pleased to hear the streets of Damascus remain quiet since our arrival in October 333 and that mighty Syria has adjusted herself to our presence.

To other matters. I write to request 4000 of your most rested troops be sent to Egypt to arrive no later than January 1 331 BC. The fighting in Gaza was bitter and our enemy merciless; my soldiers are tired and need to recuperate before marching westward.

I busy myself with the construction of the city of Alexandria. Address future correspondence to 12 Conquest Avenue Alexandria where I will soon move in order to directly oversee the construction. Deinocrates head architect has seen to every detail, but of course detail requires time. I remain here until the spring when I intend for our armies to reunite and travel west to Thapsacus Mesopotamia where we will meet Darius King of Persia and secure his defeat for our mutual triumph and to the glory of Greece!

Sincerely,

Alexander the Great (Alex)

EXERCISE 38-8 *Clarifying with Commas*

Some of the sentences in the following paragraphs are confusing because they lack clarifying commas. Add commas where readers need more clues about how to read the sentences.

Because geologists used both radiometric and fossil dating we now know that the Colorado River only started carving the Grand Canyon five or six million years ago. Scientists were able to accurately date the Shroud of Turin believed by many Catholics to be Christ's burial covering to between 1260-1390 AD This particular example of carbon dating challenged some believers to weigh faith against science. The mysterious Sphinx stands before the pyramid of Khafre dated using the "star method." Scientists determined that the Sphinx and its host pyramid are approximately seventy years younger than was originally believed.

Chapter 39

Semi-colons and Colons

EXERCISE 39-1 *Semicolon Review*

Decide where semicolons should go in the following paragraph. Add any semicolons that would repair run-on sentences, fix comma splices, or clarify a list. Also eliminate any incorrectly used semicolons, and insert the correct punctuation.

Example:

In the summer of 1947 there was a crash in eastern New Mexico; the incident feeds speculation that the government hides evidence of UFOs.

The media reported that the wreckage of a flying saucer was discovered on a ranch near Roswell however, military spokespeople came up with another explanation. They asserted that the flying saucer was actually a balloon, people stationed at the base, however, reported seeing unidentifiable bodies removed from the wreckage. Initially even ufologists believed the government's reports; which seemed plausible at the time. The Air Force has declared the case closed they stated that the bodies discovered at the crash sites were test dummies. Roswell, New Mexico joins the list of rumored UFO hotspots, including Delphos, Kansas, Marshall County, Minnesota, Westchester, New York, and Gulf Breeze, Florida.

[Source: Clark, Jerome. *The UFO Encyclopedia*: 2nd edition, Omnigraphics Inc, Detroit: 1998.]

EXERCISE 39-2 *Colon Review*

Decide where colons should go in the following paragraph; add any that are necessary. Also, eliminate any incorrectly used colons and insert correct punctuation.

Example:
Sandra Cisneros has written a number of books, including: [delete the colon] *My Wicked, Wicked Ways; Woman Hollering Creek*; and the acclaimed novel, *The House on Mango Street*.

1. *The House on Mango Street* tells the story of a Mexican American girl who has a telling name, Esperanza (Hope).

2. Because *The House on Mango Street* consists of forty-four short vignettes, critics disagree on the book's genre, autobiography, short story, novel, or poetry.

3. Whatever its genre, *The House on Mango Street* has attracted the attention of feminist and Chicano literary critics both groups appreciate the complex portrayal of racism and sexism from a young girl's perspective.

4. Cisneros dedicates the novel to women of the barrio whose stories she wants to tell; "For the ones I left behind, for the ones who cannot get out."

[Source: *Modern Women Writers*, edited by William S. Robinson. New York: Continuum, 1996.]

Chapter 40

Hyphens

In the following sentences, decide where hyphens should be placed. Some sentences may require more than one hyphen and some sentences may need hyphens deleted.

Examples:
Since there are few clear enemies of the state in the post[-]Soviet era, political parties lack a galvanizing issue.

1. Some people consider the Electoral College to be undemocratic.

2. Independent candidates are often viewed as fly by night long shots with little or no hope of winning positions of power.

3. The tension surrounding the five week wait for the 2000 presidential election results was palpable.

4. Mudslinging political ads are becoming more common.

5. Local candidates' political debates are rarely considered important enough to interrupt regularly-scheduled programming.

6. Candidates with *laissez faire* economic policies are often popular with large corporations, which in turn make substantial donations to the candidates with favorable platforms.

Chapter 41

Dashes and Parentheses

EXERCISE 41-1 *Using Punctuation for Emphasis*

Look at the complementary material and appositives that are underlined in the paragraph below. Add commas, parentheses, or dashes to set them off, based on the level of emphasis you want to create.

Example:

Coffee**,** one of the most significant crops of all time**,** has its origins in Africa **(**like so many other cornerstones of civilization**)**.

Coffea arabica the official name for the bean was made popular in Yemen. The Shadhili Sufi used coffee to inspire visions and to stimulate ecstatic trances making coffee drinking a spiritual experience. The use of the beverage spread largely through other Muslims the Sufi had contact with, and by 1500 it was well known throughout the Arab world. Cafes originated in the Middle East. These early cafes one of the few secular public spaces Muslims could congregate were seen as subversive.

[Source: *The Cambridge History of Food.* Ed. Kenneth F. Kiple and Kriemhild Conee Ornelas. Vol. 1. Cambridge University Press, 2000. 641-642.]

EXERCISE 41-2 *Setting Off Information*

Insert dashes and parentheses in the following sentences to set off information.

Example:

Naples–founded by the Greeks, enlarged by the Romans, and ruled later by the Normans, Hohenstaufen, French, and Spanish–is one of the few European cities where the links to ancient world remain evident.

1. Naples is a dirty and noisy metropolis in a spectacular setting–a city that sprawls around the Bay of Naples with Mount Vesuvius at its back facing out to the islands of Procida, Ischia, and Capri.

2. The most famous eruption of Mt. Vesuvius (the eruption that destroyed Pompeii and Herculaneum) occurred in 79 A.D.

3. The eruption came so suddenly that Pompeii was stopped in time–carbonized loaves of bread still in the oven.

4. The minor details in Pompeii–graffiti scrawled on the walls–give the city a living presence.

5. Herculaneum (also known as Ercolano) to the west of Pompeii was buried by a mudslide in the same eruption.

EXERCISE 41-3 *Parentheses Review*

Decide where to add parentheses in the following sentences. Be careful to place them correctly in relation to other punctuation marks.

> *Example:*
>
> Performing at the Grand Ole Opry **(**broadcast from Nashville, Tennessee**)** was the ultimate professional goal of all country and western hopefuls.

1. To get on the show, an artist had to have: 1 style, 2 twang, and 3 the Nashville sound.

2. The Grand Ole Opry GOO began under the name Barn Dance in 1925.

3. Historians place the Grand Ole Opry firmly within the tradition of early twentieth-century vaudeville Stambler and Landon 274.

4. The first performer was bearded fiddler Uncle Jimmy Thompson. Uncle Jimmy died in 1931.

5. In the late 1960s GOO constructed a new amphitheater complete with 4,000 seats, which became the main attraction at Opryland.

[Source: Stambler, Irwin and Grelan Landon. *The Encyclopedia of Folk, Country & Western Music.* 2nd ed. New York: St. Martin's Press, 1983. 274-75.]

Chapter 42

Apostrophes

EXERCISE 42-1 *Missing Apostrophes*

The apostrophes have been omitted from the paragraph below. Insert apostrophes in the appropriate places to indicate possession.

Example:

Pompeii's ruins were excavated during the past two centuries.

Its destruction was caused by an eruption of Mount Vesuvius in 79 AD. Survivors stories contain accounts of tunneling through up to sixteen feet of debris after the disaster. The Naples Museums collection contains painted stuccos and other art objects from Pompeii that illustrate the delicate nature of the artisans techniques. More than five hundred residents bronze seals were found, and these helped identify the occupants of many destroyed homes. Pompeiis ruins provide the worlds most accurate snapshot of Hellenistic and Roman times.

[Source: Bahr, L.S.; Bloomfield, L.A.; Johnston, B. "Pompeii." *Collier's Encyclopedia*. 1996. 233-4.]

EXERCISE 42-2 *Missing Apostrophes*

Some of the apostrophes in the paragraph below are placed correctly, some are placed incorrectly, and others are omitted altogether. Cross out incorrectly used apostrophes, and add apostrophes where necessary.

Example:

Americans have often loved their presidents' nicknames more
than they loved the ~~president's~~ presidents themselves.

1. Texas VIP's and international diplomats alike affectionately referred to Lyndon B. Johnson as Big Daddy.

126

2. There were no ifs, ands or buts when the Rough Rider, Theodore Roosevelt, rode into town.

3. Similarly, when old Give 'Em Hell, also known as Harry Truman, was on the Hill, congressmen could never catch up on their □'s.

4. Jimmy Carters staff learned quickly of his attention to small details, down to the dotting of is and crossing of ts.

5. The last twenty years have seen two George Bush's in the White House.

6. In the 1990's, George Bush Senior was known as "No New Taxes."

[Source: Hook, J.N. *All Those Wonderful Names*. New York: John Wiley and Sons, Inc., 1991. 155-156.]

Chapter 43

Quotation Marks

EXERCISE 43-1 *Quotations and Punctuation*

The sentences below contain direct quotations and paraphrases from Tony Horowitz's *Confederates in the Attic: Dispatches from the Unfinished Civil War.* Use attribution and punctuation clues to help you decide how to punctuate the quotations and paraphrases.

Example:

After completing his wild and often contradictory ride through two full years, fifteen states, and the contemporary landscape of what he terms the "South's Unfinished Civil War," award-winning journalist and cultural historian Tony Horowitz concluded: "the pleasure the Civil War gave me was hard to put into words."

1. Horowitz's difficulty was finding words that might, as he puts it, make sense to anyone but a fellow addict.

2. There are, Horowitz allows, clear and often-cited reasons why one might develop a passion for the Civil War, however. Everywhere people spoke of family and fortunes lost in the war, Horowitz writes.

3. He notes that many Southerners, nostalgic for old-time war heroism, still revere men like Stonewall Jackson, Robert E. Lee, and Nathan Bedford Forest, officers, Horowitz reminds his readers, who were often not what he calls marble-men of Southern myth.

4. Civil War heroes were, after all, human. And these men, who for some command the status of gods, were also, in Horowitz's words, petty figures who often hurt their own cause by bickering, even challenging each other to duels.

5. The Civil War was also unique because it marked the first war in which the rural landscape of the nineteenth-century United States met a new kind of war technology. As Horowitz states: It was new technology that made the War's romance and rusticity so palpable. Without photographs, rebs and Yanks would seem as remote to modern Americans as Minutemen and Hessians. Surviving daguerreotypes from the 1840's and 1850's were mostly stiff studio

portraits. So the Civil War was as far back as we could delve in our own history and bring back naturalistic images attuned to our modern way of seeing.

[Source: Horowitz, Tony. *Confederates in the Attic: Dispatches from the Unfinished Civil War*. New York: Pantheon, 1998. 84-87.]

EXERCISE 43-2 *Other Uses for Quotation Marks*

Decide whether the underlined words in the sentences below require quotation marks. Add quotation marks to indicate a novel word usage, or a word being used as a word. Delete those quotation marks that are unnecessary. Be careful not to enclose words in quotes merely for emphasis.

> *Example:*
> Biologists define "race" [*delete quotation marks*] as groups within a species that differ significantly from one another.

1. Humans have been divided into several "primary" races according to physical traits.

2. Many assume these divisions to be natural, but these natural categories are not natural at all.

3. The word race represents more than mere biological categories.

4. When politicians talk about race, for example, they often are not referring only to biological "classifications."

5. The catchword race has become a political firearm, but for such a culturally powerful concept, its meaning remains broad and unclear.

6. To talk about "race" in the U.S., however, often means to discuss contemporary racial tensions within our color-blind society.

[Source: "Race." Encyclopedia Britannica. vol. 9. 15th ed. Chicago: Encyclopedia Britannica. 876.]

EXERCISE 43-3 *Punctuation and Quotations*

The sentences below use a variety of punctuation marks with quotations. Some are used correctly and some are not. Move the punctuation marks that are incorrectly placed in relation to the quotation marks.

Example:

In her essay, "Survival Is the Least of My Desires," novelist Dorothy

Allison describes herself as "Born poor, queer, and despised[.]".
moved period inside of quotation marks

1. What does Allison mean when she tells gay and lesbian writers, "We must aim much higher than just staying alive if we are to begin to approach our true potential?"

2. She elaborates, "I want to write in such a way as to literally remake the world, to change people's thinking as they look out of the eyes of the characters I create" (212.)

3. "I believe in the truth"; this declaration forms the cornerstone of the philosophy Allison wants to pass on to gay and lesbian writers.

4. According to Allison, "I write what I think are "moral tales." That's what I intend, though I grow more and more to believe that telling the emotional truth of people's lives, not necessarily the historical truth, is the only moral use of fiction." (217)

5. "If I am to survive, I need to be able to trust your stories, to know that you will not lie even to comfort."

6. I believe the secret in writing is that fiction never exceeds the reach of the writer's courage," says Allison.

[Source: Allison, Dorothy. "Survival Is the Least of My Desires." *Skin: Talking About Sex, Class, and Literature.* Ithaca, NY: Firebrand Books, 1994. 209, 212-217.]

Chapter 44
Other Punctuation Marks

Exercise 44-1 *Periods*

Periods have been omitted from the paragraph that follows. You can see how confusing writing becomes without proper period placement. Add periods to clear up the confusion.

Example:
The origins of second wave American feminism are often traced to Ms[.] Betty Friedan of Peoria, Ill[.]

Ms Friedan was born Feb 4, 1921 History will record her as one of the major contributors to modern US feminism In 1963, Friedan penned the monumental *Feminine Mystique* The book investigated the contemporary malaise of the postwar US housewife which she dubbed "the problem that has no name" Friedan spoke for the millions of housewives who were wondering why they were discontent as mothers and wives In 1966, she co-founded the National Organization of Women (NOW was co-conceptualized by African American feminist/minister Pauli Murray at the 1966 National Conference of the Commission on the Status of Women in Washington DC). Friedan went on to serve as president of NOW (wwwnoworg) until 1970, and she has since published works such as *It Changed My Life, The Second Stage, Life So Far,* etc
[Source: *Encarta Encyclopedia Website.*
<http://encarta.msn.com/find/Concise.asp?ti=038AC000> 24 Jul 2001.]

EXERCISE 44-2 *Missing Punctuation*

Periods and question marks have been omitted from the paragraph that follows. Place them where they are needed.

Example:
What was so Earth-shattering about Friedan's naming of the "problem with no name"[?]

131

Betty Friedan's *The Feminine Mystique* addressed the question, "Is this all" She examined why millions of women were sensing a gnawing feeling of discontent Friedan asked, "Can the problem that has no name somehow be related to the domestic routine of the housewife" and examined women's shifting place in postwar America What were women missing In a major move for the feminist movement, Friedan legitimized the panic and uneasiness of many women who found the roles of mother and wife not wholly satisfying However, did this naming solve the "problem with no name"

[Source: Friedan, Betty. *The Feminine Mystique.* New York: W.W Norton, 1963. 15-16, 30.]

EXERCISE 44-3 *Punctuation and Elliptical Phrasing*

Below are quotations of prose and AE Houseman's poem "To An Athlete Dying Young." Delete the underlined passages and punctuate the quotes with ellipses where necessary. Be sure to leave in clarifying punctuation.

Example:

Robert Ward states, "The American culture positions its heroes such that they are destined to end in turmoil, problematizing the desire for eminent success. By elevating them to the position of gods, society gives heroes no where to go but down."

Robert Ward states, "The American culture positions its heroes such that they are destined to end in turmoil . . . . By elevating them to the position of gods, society gives heroes no where to go but down."

Ward notes, "The phenomenon of the waning star is heavily represented in the last century of English and American culture, ranging from poetry to popular rock music." In 1896, chronicling the advantage of dying before the glory fades, A.E. Houseman published the poem "To an Athlete Dying Young." The following is a passage from that poem:

Now you will not swell the rout

Of lads that wore their honors out,

Runners whom renown outran

And the name died before the man

So set, before the echoes fade,

The fleet foot on the sill of shade,

And hold to the low lintel up

The still-defended challenge-cup.

And round that early-laureld head

Will flock to gaze the strengthless dead

And find unwithered on its curls

The garland briefer than a girl's.

Houseman's verses extol the eternal glory of one who passes in his/her prime. Scholars such as Ona Click have noted the recent proliferation of Houseman's theme, citing that "artists such as Neil Young have contemporized this notion with songs such as 'Hey Hey My My.' The song contrasts the fates two rock stars who ultimately took two very different paths, Elvis Presley and Johnny Rotten of the Sex Pistols; while Presley died in a blaze of glory, Rotten's fleeting stardom waned and dulled the cultural memory of his initial rise to fame." In a related article, she notes this theme traveled into the 1980s as Bruce Springsteen's "Glory Days" recalled the tale of "those who outlive their primes and are forced to reduce their glory to nostalgic reminiscences and fleeting grasps at the past." Though we venerate our heroes, culture notes how their position is tenuous at best.

[Source: A.E. Houseman. "To an Athlete Dying Young." *The McGraw-Hill Book of Poetry*. Eds. Robert DiYanni and Draft Rofpf. New York: McGraw-Hill, 1983. 499-500.]

EXERCISE 44-4 *Punctuation Review*

Take a look at the way the following paragraph uses all the punctuation marks discussed in this chapter: periods, question marks, exclamation points, brackets, ellipses, and slashes. Some are used correctly, and others are used incorrectly or omitted altogether. Correct any mistakes with punctuation that you find, and add any necessary marks that have been omitted.

Example:

Many ask, "Why have snakes become a symbol of religious devotion?"

In 1996 alone, over sixty deaths occurred due to religious snake handling. Mark 16-21 in the King James version of The Bible states, "They shall take up serpents and if they drink the deadly thing it shall not hurt them . . ."! This passage instigated the formation of a religion which thrives within the Irish and English descendants living in Appalachia. (In the 1990s, over 2000 snake handlers lived in Appalachia alone.)

Snake handling has been investigated by both the fine arts (Romulus Linney's "Holy Ghosts" (1971) examines snake handling in the South) and news media. One controversial case examined Rev Glenn Summerford who attempted to kill his wife by forcing her to handle rattlesnakes. The general public often sees snake handling as a frightening act of fundamentalism practiced by congregations (often assumed to be undereducated)

Chapter 45

Write with Accurate Spelling

EXERCISE 45-1 *Spelling*

After writing the paragraph below, the writer ran it through a spell checker and took all of the checker's advice. The checker missed some errors and created a few new errors. Correct all the spelling mistakes in the paragraph.

> *Example:*
>
> It's ~~Its~~ indicative of ~~Despond~~ Desmond Tutu's feelings of solidarity with his
>
> parishioners that he opted to live in ~~Sowed~~ Soweto, a poor black
>
> neighborhood, rather than in Houghton, a rich suburb.

Archbishop Despond Tutu's message to the peoples of South Africa is that all are of infinite worth, created in the image of god, and to be treated with reverence. Tutu maintains that this is true fore whites as well as blacks, a position that isn't popular wit some South African. It can be scene from the many awards tutu has received, not least among them the Nobel Peace Prize in 1984, that his commitment to morality and human freedom have had an effect the world over. Archbishop Despond Tutu is a ban who does not waist the potential of hiss powerful role as religious leader. On the contrary, the Archbishop seas many political problems as moral ones and speaks out frequently on human rights issues.

[Source: Wepman, Dennis. *Desmond Tutu*. New York: Franklin Watts, 1989. 13-15, 62-65.]

EXERCISE 45-2 *Homophones*

Underline the correct homophones in the paragraph that follows.

Example:
(<u>Except</u>/Accept) for the ethnic cleansings in Rwanda in 1995, one of the worst incidents of genocide in history occurred in the South East Asia country of Cambodia.

Modern day Cambodia, or Kampuchea, gained its independence from France in 1953, but (by/buy) the early 1970s the country was embroiled in bloody civil war. In 1975, Khmer Rouge guerrillas secured the Cambodian (Capital/capitol), Phnom Phen, (where/wear) they ruled the country until 1979. Once in power, the Khmer Rouge killed over 25% of their fellow Cambodians; (all together/altogether) they murdered over 2 million people. Most of those killed met their deaths at a (sight/site) (write/right) outside of Phnom Phen, known today as the "Killing Fields". The (affects/effects) of the Khmer Rouge's brief, yet defining rule remain all (to/too) apparent in contemporary Cambodia.

[Source: Encyclopedia of World Conflicts]

EXERCISE 45-3 *Adding Suffixes*

Each of the root words below ends in a consonant-vowel-consonant combination. Write the correct spelling of each word with the addition of the suffix.

Example:
　occur + ed = occurred
　stop + ing = stopping

1. slap + ed = _____

2. refer + ing = _____

3. drop + ed = _____

4. ship + ment = _____

5. dim + er = _____

6. run + ing = _____

7. refer + ence = _____

8. benefit + ed = _____

9. commit + ment = _____

10. forget + able = _____

EXERCISE 45-4 *Adding Suffixes to Silent E's*

Each of the root words below ends in a silent *e*. Write the correct spelling of each word with the addition of the suffix. Pay attention to whether the first letter of the suffix is a consonant or a vowel.

Example:
   continue + ous = continuous
   state + ly = stately

1. definite + ly = _____

2. pure + ist = _____

3. spine + less = _____

4. exercise + ing = _____

5. imagine + ation = _____

6. hate + ful = _____

7. judge + ment = _____

8. debate + able = _____

9. like + able = _____

10. nine + th = _____

EXERCISE 45-5 *Plurals*

In the following paragraph, words that should be plural, but are singular, are underlined. Make all the underlined words plural. Where necessary, change verbs so that they agree with the plural words.

Example:

Why Oscar Wilde, in 1885, brought Lord Queensbury to trial

on charges of libel remains one of the great <u>mystery</u> _{*mysteries*}

of literary history.

     Wilde, a successful author with two <u>child</u> and multiple <u>follower</u> in literary London, made a mistake when he pressed <u>charge</u> against the famous lord. By all <u>account</u>, Wilde was in jovial <u>spirit</u> when he arrived at the Old Bailey courthouse on April 3, 1895. <u>Passerby</u> may have seen the famous writer make one of his characteristically fantastic <u>entrance</u>: Wilde's carriage was outfitted with two <u>horse,</u> several <u>servant,</u> and all the pomp and circumstance his public character demanded. But the series of <u>event</u> that followed led up to one of the great <u>crash</u> of the Victorian era. Wilde lost the libel suit and was then himself tried, twice, based on <u>body</u> of evidence amassed against him in the first trial. The <u>medium</u> was not sympathetic to Wilde, who had come to embody the multiple <u>threat</u> of moral indecency for conservative <u>Victorian</u>. In the <u>day</u> following his two <u>trial</u> and ultimate conviction for the newly-illegal crime of Gross Indecency, both print <u>article</u> and <u>caricature</u> presenting <u>story</u> from the trial served as <u>knife</u> in the artist's back. Wilde was sentenced to two <u>year</u> "hard labor," and upon his release from prison fled to France in exile. He died two <u>year</u> later. Wilde lived two <u>life</u> in his brief 47 years; he lived the first under the spotlight of fame, and the second under the glare of infamy. But his <u>philosophy</u> of art and beauty survive, as Wilde predicted they would.

[Source: Ellmann, Richard. *Oscar Wilde*]

EXERCISE 45-6 *Spelling Rules*

Words in the following paragraph illustrate all the rules explained in Section 31c, Learn Spelling Rules. Some are spelled correctly and some are spelled incorrectly. Rewrite any words that are spelled incorrectly.

Their are several kinds of sleep disorders, the most common being insomnia. Sleepyness during daytime hours can often be a sign of needing more rest during the night. Insomnia is defined as a disatisfaction with the amount or quality of sleep aquired. It is interesting to note that many people who identifeid themselves as insomniacs for a study were found to be awake less than 30 min. per night. It is possable that these test subjects were sleeping lightly and suffered from a lack of "good" sleep. There are a number of sugestions for increasing your chances of getting proper sleep. First, stick to a scedule. Even on weekends it is a good idea to rise at the same time as during the week. Second, avoid alcohol and stimulants such as caffeine. Alchohol can disturb sleep cycles and even a small amount of caffeine can remain in the blood stream for a long period of time. Regular exercise can actually help sleeping, but a workout right before bed sresses your chances of good sleep. Perhaps the most important criteeria for proper sleep is relaxation. Meditative exerciese or relaxing music can reduce stress and help get you ready for restfull sleep. Also, reserch actually supports the old tale that a warm glass of milk before bed can help you get a good nights sleep.

[Source: Atkinson, Rita L., et al. *Introduction to Psychology Eleventh Edition*. Fort Worth: Harcourt Brace College Publishers, 1993. p. 214-5.]

EXERCISE 46-1 *Capitalization Review*

Nothing in the paragraph that follows has been capitalized. Revise as necessary.

> *Example:*
> courses in american history often disregard the founding of the fbi.
> Courses in American history often disregard the founding of the FBI.

the federal bureau of investigation (fbi) has long been considered an american institution that was fathered by president theodore roosevelt. during the early 1900s, the united states was going through what some referred to as the progressive era. (during this period, the american people believed government intervention was synonymous with a just society.) roosevelt, the president during part of this era, aided in the creation of an organization devoted to federal investigations. prior to 1907, federal investigations were carried out by agents-for-hire employed by the department of justice. on wednesday, may 27, 1908, the u.s. congress passed a law prohibiting the employment of agents-for-hire and enabling the establishment of an official secret service directly affiliated with the department. that spring, attorney general charles bonaparte appointed ten agents who would report to a chief examiner. this action is often considered to be the birth of the fbi.

[Source: *Official FBI Website.* <http://www.fbi.gov/fbiinbrief/historic/history> 26 Jul 2001.]

EXERCISE 46-2 *When to Italicize*

Underline any words in the following paragraph that should be italicized.

Example:

Both controversial in their own right, famed clothing designer Coco Chanel and the painter of <u>Guernica</u>, Pablo Picasso, are listed by <u>Time</u> magazine as two of the "Most Interesting People of the Twentieth Century."

Many think Coco Chanel is to fashion what the Bible is to religion. Consequently, various types of media have sought to capture the essence of this innovative designer. Films such as Tonight or Never preserve Chanel's designs for future generations, while the failed Broadway musical Coco attempts to embody her life's work. More recently, print and small screen have attempted to encapsulate the impact of the designer in specials like A&E Top 10: Fashion Designers and books such as Chanel: Her Style and Her Life. Chanel was as monumental and self-destructive as the Titanic. She almost single-handedly redefined women's clothing through the popularization of sportswear and the jersey suit. But she also sympathized with Hitler after the release of his book Mein Kampf and the relocation of the Jews, and her image was further tarnished by her wartime romance with a Nazi officer. However, after her initial success waned during World War II, magazines such as Vogue and Life welcomed her back. She reinvented herself and her clothing line in the 1950s, and today she stands as one of the most influential fashion designers in history.

[Source: *Time Magazine Official Website.*
<http://www.time.com/time/time100/artists/profile/chanel3.html> 26 Jul 2001.
Internet Movie Database. <http://imdb.com> 26 Jul 2001. Wallach, Janet.
Chanel: Her Style and Her Life. New York: Doubleday, 1998. 150.]

Chapter 47
Abbreviations, Acronyms, and Numbers

EXERCISE 47-1 *Deciding When to Abbreviate*

The following is a paragraph from a research paper in which every word is spelled out. Decide which words would be more appropriate as abbreviations and write them correctly. Remember, this is formal academic writing; be sure to follow the conventions for using abbreviations in papers. When you have more than one abbreviation style to choose from, select the one recommended in this section. Note: the term "dense rock equivalent" is abbreviated DRE.

> *Example:*
>
> Ph.D.
> Peter Francis, ~~Doctor of Philosophy~~ is among the scholars who have written introductory texts on volcanoes.

The unpredictable, destructive nature of volcanoes has attracted the interest of both scholarly and lay circles. Though it erupted in 79 anno Domini, Mount Vesuvius is still famous because of its violent decimation of the city of Pompeii. Second to Vesuvius in destructive power is Mount Pelée, which in 1902 killed nearly thirty thousand people (id est, all but four of the citizens of Saint Pierre). Scholars like Professor George Walker have attempted to quantify and predict the effects of volcanoes. Professor Walker developed a system whereby volcanoes are judged by magnitude, intensity, dispersive power, violence, and destructive potential. Walker began using a measurement called dense rock equivalent to measure unwitnessed eruptions. The actual volume of a volcano is converted into dense rock equivalent, which accounts for spaces in the rocks. Walker et alia have continued to perform research which will aid in the study of volcanoes.

[Source: Woodhead, James. *Geology.* Vol. 2. Pasadena and Hackensack: Salem Press, Inc., 1999. 677, 684, 686.]

EXERCISE 47-2 *Using Acronyms Correctly*

The following paragraph from a research paper uses some acronyms correctly and some incorrectly. Revise the paragraph, adding acronyms where needed and spelling out the words where needed. You may also need to add or subtract punctuation marks such as parentheses and periods. Please refer to the list below for the relevant acronyms. Remember, you make decisions based on whether or not the general population is familiar with the acronym.

UNDAT - United Nations Declaration Against Torture
LAPD - Los Angeles Police Department
KKK - Ku Klux Klan
DEA - Drug Enforcement Agency
IRA - Irish Republican Army
CIA - Central Intelligence Agency
SERE - Survival, Evasion, Resistance, and Escape
HRC - Human Rights Campaign
ACLU - American Civil Liberties Union

Example:

LAPD

In 1992, the ~~Los Angeles Police Department~~ was accused of unduly torturing an African-American motorist, Rodney King.

Various organizations define torture in different ways; however, UNDAT officially defines torture as undue pain suffered at the hands of a public official. Despite the various definitions, however, the general public knows torture when it sees it. From Ku Klux Klan lynchings to the torture of American DEA agents by the Mexican government, torture is alive and well in the American consciousness. Though we often associate torture with medieval times or extremist groups such as the I.R.A., America's Central Intelligence Agency has been accused of using torture as a method of coercion. Torture is so present in the world that the U.S. armed forces put their personnel through a special training program – SERE. SERE theoretically prepares soldiers to survive torture. Because of the prevalence of torture in what are generally considered civilized societies, organizations such as HRC and the ACLU fight to preserve the rights of those who cannot protect themselves.

[Source: Gottesman, Ronald and Richard Maxwell Brown. *Violence in America.* New York: Charles Scribner's Sons, 1999. 333-336.]

EXERCISE 47-3 *Word-Numbers or Numerals*

All of the numbers in the following paragraph are spelled out. Decide where it would be more appropriate to use the numerals instead and revise. Remember to add hyphens where necessary.

> *Example:*
> Caused by the dysfunction of two tiny joints near the ears, a
>
> form of TMJ (temporomandibular joint dysfunction) was
>   1934
> identified in ~~nineteen hundred thirty-four~~ by Doctor Costen.

Five hundred sixty is the number of times you heard a popping sound resonating from the jaw of the woman sitting next to you on the plane. She may be one of over nine point five million people suffering from TMJ, a condition that often causes symptoms such as popping, swelling, and aching in the jaw. At least one study has shown that women on hormone treatments are seventy seven percent more likely to develop TMJ symptoms. The disorder goes by at least six names, most of which include the initials TM for temporomandibular: Costen's Syndrome, TMJ, TMD, TMJDD, CMD, and TMPD. Doctors currently prescribe at least forty nine different treatments for the disorder, ranging from one dollar and fifty cent mouth guards to prevent tooth grinding to a myriad of treatments which could cost thousands of dollars.

[Source: *TMJ Association Official Website.* <http://www.tmj.org> 27 Jul 2001.]

Chapter 48

Writing in a Second Language

EXERCISE 48-1 *Understand How Languages Differ*

Write a few paragraphs describing your language and literacy backgrounds. In what language did you first learn to write? When you write, which language do you use to develop and organize ideas? When you write, which language do you use and in what situations? In which language have you done your best writing? How would you compare the experience of writing in your first and second languages?

Chapter 49

Nouns and Articles

EXERCISE 49-1 *Common Nouns*

Underline the common nouns in the paragraph below once and underline the proper nouns twice. Correct any errors in capitalization.

Example:

                Chicago   laws

In 1903, a <u>fire</u> in <u>chicago</u> led to the new safety <u>Laws</u> .

In 1903, Chicago opened the new iroquois theater on West Randolph street. Around christmas, the Theater held a performance of "mr. blue beard" starring eddie Foy. Shortly after the play started, a light sparked causing a curtain to catch on fire. Elvira Pinedo said the crowd panicked after a giant Fireball appeared. This panic led to the deaths of nearly five hundred people, many of whom died because bodies were pressed against doors that opened inward. Shortly after the Tragedy, mayor Carter h. Harrison was indicted and new laws demanded Theaters have doors that open outward, toward the lobby.

[Source: Jimenez, Gilbert. "Fire Issues in New City Fire Code." *Chicago Sun Times* Website <http://www.suntimes.com/century/m1903.html> 20 Oct 2001.]

EXERCISE 49-2 *Plural Nouns*

The following sentences include various types of plural nouns: count, noncount, and those that can be either, depending upon how they are used. Underline the correct plural form from the choices provided.

Example:

Barry Gordy's Motown Records made (<u>much money</u>/monies) and introduced America to (many entertainer, <u>entertainers</u>) who would have otherwise been silenced because of their race.

1. In the late 1950s, Detroit was one of America's (many city, cities) famous for the production of (numbers of automobile, automobiles).

2. Detroit's sound soon changed from the auto industry's assembly line of heavy (pieces of equipment, equipments) to Motown's assembly line of superstar musical (groups of act/acts).

3. Gordy was famous for his (kinds of method/methods) of production; he tailored images down to the styles of performers' (hair/hairs), dances, and musical numbers.

4. The (positions of employment/employments) were clear; (all of the employee/employees) were allowed to perform only the tasks for which they were specifically hired.

5. Though Gordy's techniques led Motown to (much wealth/wealths), the same techniques sent entertainers packing for labels that would provide them with (more personal satisfaction/personal satisfactions).

6. The apartment is unfurnished; you may need to buy (a few pieces of furniture/some furnitures).

[Source: Stern, Jane and Michael Stern. *Encyclopedia of Pop Culture* (New York: Harper Perennial, 1992) 339-342.]

EXERCISE 49-3 *Singular/Plural Inconsistencies*

The following paragraph includes many examples of singular/plural inconsistency. Correct any incorrect versions of nouns.

Example:

> words
>
> In the history of fashion, many word have lost their original
> meanings
> meaning.

Every year, thousands of bride and groom don traditional attire while attending their wedding. one garment associated with many of these traditional wedding is the groom's cummerbund or decorative waistband. This garment dates back many century to Persia where grooms would wrap their loin in a tight cotton cloth called a "kamarband" or "loin band". This cloth was meant to display the genitals for the various bride-to-be. By the time many British settler inhabited the Middle East, the original meaning of the tradition had disappeared, and like a number of garment, it was being worn strictly as decoration.

[Source: Panati, Charles. Sexy Origins and Intimate Things (New York: Penguin Books, 1998) 338.]

EXERCISE 49-4 *Choosing the Right Article*

Underline the correct definite or indefinite article for the nouns in the paragraph below.

> *Example:*
> Both (a/an/the) novel and (a/an/the) screenplay have been written about the career of (a/an/the) African American boxer Jack Johnson.

In (a/an/the) early 1900s, boxing films were (a/an/the) extremely popular form of entertainment; (a/an/the) fight would be filmed and shown in movie houses across (a/an/the) country. This practice changed after (a/an) race riot occurred following (a/an) match between (a/an/the) white man, ex-champion Jim Jeffries, and (a/an/the) black man, Jack Johnson. Jeffries had previously refused to fight (a/an) African American boxer, but after Johnson defeated (a/an/the) current white champion, Jeffries agreed to meet (a/an/the) challenger. After Johnson defeated (a/an/the) ex-champion, a nationwide race riot erupted in large portions of (a/an/the) south, as well as (a/an/the) number of other locales. These riots caused (a/an/the) alarm in (a/an/the) United States Congress, and within three weeks, (a/an) bill was passed prohibiting (a/an/the) public screening of such films.

[Source: Bederman, Gail. *Manliness and Civilization: A Cultural History of Gender and Race in the United States, 1880-1917* (Chicago: University of Chicago Press, 1995) 2-3.]

EXERCISE 49-5 *Article Review*

The following paragraph includes several examples of properly and improperly used articles. Underline articles, identify types of nouns they modify (plural or singular count or noncount), and correct any improperly chosen articles.

Example:

      The/singular count   an/singular count
      Just after <u>an</u> end of American involvement in <u>a</u> unpopular war,
    the/plural count   the/singular count
    one of <u>a</u> most quirky fads of <u>a</u> Twentieth Century
          noncount   singular count
    brought piles of <u>a</u> money to <u>an</u> American advertising agent.

    While Americans recovered from a Vietnam War, Gary Dahl sat in the California restaurant talking with friends. Dahl joked of the inconveniences of the traditional pets owned by his buddies; this conversation produced the brainchild that would bring him much a wealth and satisfaction. His idea was to maintain the fun of the live pet in the form of a unique pet rock: a rock, training manual, and carrying case. By the mid-seventies, buying your girlfriend pieces of a jewelry had been replaced by the popular Pet Rock. A curiosity made the news and earned Dahl millions of dollars.

[Source: Stern, Jane and Michael Stern. *Encyclopedia of Pop Culture* (New York: Harper Perennial, 1992) 379-381]

EXERCISE 50-1 *To Be or Not To Be*

The following paragraph is filled with "be" verbs. In each case, underline the correct verb form from the choices provided in parentheses.

Example:

> Rosh Hashanah, one of the religious High Holy Days, (is celebrated/ is celebrating) during the second day of the seventh month of the Jewish colander, Tishri.

Though many think it simply marks the Jewish New Year, Rosh Hashanah actually (was conceiving/ was conceived) with a four-fold meaning. Those who celebrate the day (believe/ are believing) it stands to represent the New Year, as well as days of Shofar blowing, remembrance, and judgment. It long (has been consider/ has been considered) the only High Holy Day that warrants a two-day celebration; those who (observe/ are observing) the holiday consider the two-day period one extended forty-eight hour day. As families feast, the foods they (eat/ are eating) (are sweetened/ are sweetening) with honey, apples, and carrots, symbolizing the sweet year to come. Challah, the bread that (is eating/ is eaten) on the Sabbath, is reshaped into a ring, symbolizing the upcoming year will roll smoothly.

[Source: "The Jewish Holiday of Rosh Hashanah." http://www.holidays.net/highholydays/rosh.htm. 4 Nov 2001.]

EXERCISE 50-2 *Modal Auxiliary Verbs*

The following sentences contain modal auxiliary verbs. Some are used properly and some improperly. Underline the modal auxiliary verbs and identify what they express based on the 10 possibilities listed in this chapter (speculation, ability, necessity, etc.). Please correct any incorrect modal usage.

Example:

                                    might be/possibility

> The cause of Karen Silkwood's death <u>might could being</u> one of the great conspiracy theories of recent American history.

1. In the 1970s, the Kerr-McGee plutonium plant was accused of violations that may shall have endangered workers' lives.

2. After becoming contaminated with airborne plutonium, Karen Silkwood decided she would working harder to affect change.

3. Silkwood believed she had information that should have gone public and would having incriminated the company.

4. On the day she would have shared her information, she died in an automobile accident.

5. Some think her death might have been part of a conspiracy carried out by the company.

[Source: Kohn, Howard. "Malignant Giant." *20 Years of Rolling Stone: What a Long Strange Trip It's Been.* Ed. Jann Wenner (New York: Friendly Press, 1987) 230-245.]

EXERCISE 50-3 *Missing Parts of Sentences*

Complete the following sentences by choosing the proper verb, pronoun, and infinitive combinations from those provided in the parentheses. Underline the correct answer.

Example:

Many Slavic myths (to advise you/<u>advise you to</u>) reevaluate the significance of nature.

1. The evil Koshchei the Deathless would attempt (you to hide/to hide) under a giant oak tree.

2. The goddess of death Baba Yaga would (cause to turn victims/cause her victims to turn) into stone.

3. Hiding in corn, field spirits called Poleviks would make drunken farm workers (fear/to fear) for their lives.

4. You can prepare (heed/to heed) earth goddess Mati-Syra-□emlya by digging a hole and listening for her advice.

5. Rusalkas, souls of infants or drowned girls, could (order you to die/order to die you) a watery death with their songs.

[Source: Wilkinson, Phillip. *Illustrated Dictionary of Mythology* (New York: DK Publishing, 1998) 88-89.]

EXERCISE 50-4 *Verbs + Gerunds or Infinitives*

The following sentences include verbs that should be followed by either gerunds or infinitives. Please underline the correct gerund or infinitive from the options provided in parentheses. If both options are correct, underline both.

Example:
Some will suggest (to research/<u>researching</u>) folklore is a difficult task.

1. Historians risk (misidentifying/to misidentify) actual origins when stories have been passed down simply by word of mouth.

2. Though some like (to believe/believing) Edward O'Reilly found the story of Pecos Bill circulating amongst American cowboys, it is hard to prove.

3. The story of little Bill who was raised by wolves fails (to fade/fading) away despite its ambiguous origins.

4. Despite the confusion, Bill's bride Slue-Foot Sue and horse Widow Maker continue (to spread/spreading) as part of Americana.

5. Because of the debate over authenticity, however, some consider (to call/calling) the story popular culture, rather than folklore.

[Source: Brunvand, Jan Harold. "Pecos Bill." *Microsoft Encarta Encyclopedia Standard 2001.*]

EXERCISE 50-5 *Conditional Categories*

Rewrite the following sentences to reflect the conditional category represented in the parentheses following the sentence.

Example:

If you were to browse through the twentieth century culture, you discover many phrases used to describe human mating rituals. (predictive)

If you were to browse through the twentieth century culture, you would discover many phrases used to describe human mating rituals.

1. If a fraternity boy wanted to become engaged to his girlfriend, he pin his fraternity pin on her blouse. (factual)

2. When a turn of the century male wanted to schedule an appointment with his love, he make a "date." (factual)

3. If you had bruised the neck of your partner in the 1920s, you blame the "doo-hickey" on a rope burn or the like. (hypothetical)

4. If you cannot afford to buy your own car and fuel, you find "double dating" more economical. (predictive)

5. If you had been accused of "necking" in the North, you accuse with "petting" in the South. (hypothetical)

[Source: Panati, Charles. *Sexy Origins and Intimate Things* (New York: Penguin Books, 1998) 160.]

EXERCISE 50-6 *Participle Adjectives*

The following paragraph is filled with participial adjectives. Underline each participial adjective once and the word being modified twice.

Example:

The <u>whirling</u> <u>tornado</u> is often considered one of the world's most

<u>damaging</u> natural <u>disasters</u>.

Many tornadoes are created by a special rotating thunderstorm called a supercell. A rising gust of warm wind combines with the raging storm; however, the warm air is converted as the rainfall causes a rushing downdraft. This interaction creates a harrowing twister that is awful for those in its path. The United States is honored to bear the devastating distinction of hosting the world's most tornadoes per year; homeowners in the regions known as "Tornado Alley" and "Dixie Alley" are mortified when they see the funneling tornado making a terrifying beeline for their houses.

[Source: Shapiro, Alan. "Tornadoes." Microsoft Encarta Encyclopedia Standard 2001.]

Chapter 51

English Sentence Structure

EXERCISE 51-1 *Subjects in Sentences*

Underline all of the subjects in the following sentences. Some may have more than one subject; some may appear to have none. If the sentence appears to have no subject, supply the needed expletive.

> *Example:*
> Though <u>you</u> may have heard of Lee Harvey Oswald and John Wilkes Booth, many lesser known <u>individuals</u> have put presidents in harm's way.

1. Though some assassins are widely known, Charles Guiteau and Leon Czolgolsz are relatively obscure.
2. Guiteau shot President Garfield in 1881, and was little doubt he would be hung for the murder.
3. Twenty years later, Czolgolsz stood face to face with his victim, President William McKinley.
4. History books are littered with names of attempted assassins such as Giuseppe ☐angara, Samuel Byck, and Sarah Jane Moore.
5. You should protect your leaders, because is no way to tell what the future will bring.

[Source: *Assassins* Original Cast Recording. CD sleeve liner notes. 7-8.]

EXERCISE 51-2 *Independent Clauses*

In the following paragraph, underline independent clauses once and dependent clauses twice. Circle the subjects in each.

Example:

> When scientists explain phenomena such as volcanoes and earthquakes, they often use the theory of plate tectonics.

1. Geologists based the theory on an earlier one that had observed that the continents fit together like pieces of a puzzle.
2. In the fifties and sixties, scientists found evidence to support the earlier theory, so they were able to confirm its hypothesis regarding continental drift.
3. Though water and earth appear to be distinctly separate, they share a similar under layer called the asthenosphere.

4. This asthenosphere possesses high temperatures and pressures, and these conditions allow for fluid rock movement.
5. As plates move around, they can create volcanoes or increase and decrease the size of oceans and mountains.

[Source: "Plate Tectonics."*Microsoft® Encarta® Encyclopedia 2001.*]

EXERCISE 51-3 *Labeling Parts of Sentences*

Label the following in the sentences below: subject (S), transitive or intransitive verb (TV or IV), linking verb (LV), direct object (DO), indirect object (IO), subject compliment (SC), and prepositional phrase (PP). Not all sentences will contain ALL of these parts, but all will contain some.

Example:

   S   TV   DO   PP   PP

    Hinduism includes several gods and heroes in its system of beliefs.

1. Ganesh is the god of good luck.

2. Young Ganesh stood at his mother's house.

3. He denied his father entry.

4. His father beheaded him.

5. His mother replaced his head with the head of an elephant.

[Source: Wilkinson, Phillip. *Illustrated Dictionary of Mythology* (New York: DK Publishing, 1998) 40.]

EXERCISE 51-4 *Confusing Modifiers*

The following sentences include confusing modifiers. Underline the confusing modifiers, identify the broken rule (far away from modified word, adverb between verb and direct object, adverbial phrase between subject and verb, split infinitive), and rewrite the sentence clearly.

Example:

Japanese film often is defined by the work of Akira Kurosawa <u>worldwide</u>. [Far away from modified word]

Japanese film often is defined worldwide by the work of Akira Kurosawa.

1. Kurosawa chose initially painting as his preferred career.

2. Kurosawa, realizing painting would not bring riches, turned to film in 1936.

3. He was able to by 1943 direct his own films.

4. He is remembered for his Samurai films by many.

5. Many of his films, embraced in the West, retold Shakespearean tales.

[Source: Smyth, Eileen. "Biography of Akira Kurosawa." <u>http://www.foreignfilms.com/bio.asp?person_id=1032</u>. 10 Nov 2001.]

EXERCISE 51-5 *Correct Placement of Adjectives and Adverbs*

Each of the following sentences includes at least one adjective and adverb, some placed correctly and some incorrectly. Underline all adjectives and adverbs. Label adverbs of manner or adverbs of frequency, and correct any improper word order.

Example:

adverb of frequency

Americans associate <u>often</u> cards and dice with <u>shady</u> gamblers <u>Las Vegas</u>.

Often, Americans associate cards and dice with shady Las Vegas gamblers.

1. By the fourteenth century, early cards playing were used widely for gambling and predicting the future.

2. The invention of the printing press directly connects to the proliferation of card games standardized.

3. Ancient dice directly can be traced to Tutankhamen's tomb.

4. Gamblers hollowed frequently the center of an illegally rigged die.

5. These classic games have withstood well the test of time.

[Source: Cunningham, Lawrence and John Reich, *Culture and Values: A Survey of the Western Humanities* (Fort Worth: Hartcourt Brace College Publishers, 1994) 353.]

EXERCISE 51-6 *Dangling Modifiers*

The following sentences include dangling modifiers. Rewrite the sentences so that the relationship between subject, verb, and modifier is clear.

Example:

>   In his early thirties, France was dealt a hefty blow by Maximilien Robespierre.
>
>   In his early thirties, Maximilien Robespierre dealt France a hefty blow.

1. His philosophical role model, Robespierre followed the writings of Jean Jacques Rousseau.

2. Elected on the eve of the French Revolution, the people were enthralled by his skillful oratory.

3. Gaining further power in the following years, his influence over domestic affairs was unmistakable.

4. A bloodbath known as the Reign of Terror, Robespierre ordered a rash of executions of members of the aristocracy and his political enemies

5. After they tired of his aggressive tactics, he was overthrown by his own political party.

[Source: "Robespierre, Maximilien François Marie Isidore de."*Microsoft® Encarta® Encyclopedia 2001.*]

Chapter 52
Idiomatic Structures

EXERCISE 52-1 *Preposition Review*

Underline the proper preposition in parentheses in the following paragraph.

Example:

(<u>In</u>, On, At) the 1940s, several dozen pilots died trying to break mach one, the speed of sound.

(In, On, At) this time, pilots were familiar (with, in, on) the "Wall of Air" that existed (in, on, at) the speed of sound. Many airplanes shattered (into, onto, from) a million pieces because of this "Wall of Air." Pilots were especially afraid (for, on, of) a condition called "compressibility" which would make them lose control (in, of, on) the plane. Air Force pilot Chuck Yeager tried to break the sound barrier (from, with, on) "Glamorous Glennis," a plane named (from, for, to) his wife. (In, On, At) October 14th, 1947, Yeager made an attempt to reach mach one. The ground crew heard a boom (from, at, in) the distance and feared that "Glamorous Glennis" had crashed. They cheered (with, from, in) joy when they heard Yeager (with, in, on) the radio a few moments later saying he had broken the sound barrier.
[Source: *Mach 1.0 and Beyond.* http://www.capstonestudio.com/supersonic]

EXERCISE 52-2 *Adjective-preposition Phrases*

The paragraph below contains adjective-preposition phrases. Underline the correct preposition.

Example:

The Statue of Liberty was (full for/<u>full of</u>) significance for the millions of immigrants.

The United States remains (grateful to/grateful with) the people of France for the gift of the Statue of Liberty. France supported the colonists during the American Revolution and continues to be (proud for/proud of) its role in creating the United States. Although many Americans today are not (aware of/aware with) the importance of French support in the founding of their country, they are nonetheless (interested in/interested with) French culture and (fond of/fond with) its cuisine.

Chapter 1

EXERCISE 1-1 *Persuasive Appeals*

1. credibility

EXERCISE 1-2 *A Writer's Audience*

No to some information, neutral attitude, low interest.

EXERCISE 1-3 *A Writer's Ethos*

1. I was sub-divisional police officer of the town. [A ranking police officer is assumed to have good, specific knowledge of his community.]

Chapter 2

EXERCISE 2-1 *Images*

Answer will vary

EXERCISE 2-2 *Words or Visuals?*

1. text

EXERCISE 2-3 *For Practice: Words and Visuals*

Answer will vary

Chapter 3

EXERCISE 3-1 *Planning*

Answers will vary.

EXERCISE 3-2 *Finding a Topic*

Answers will vary.

EXERCISE 3-3 *Exploring the Topic*

Answers will vary.

EXERCISE 3-4 *Reflective, Informative, Persuasive*

1. reflective

EXERCISE 3-5 *Creating the Thesis*

Answers will vary.

EXERCISE 3-6 *Evaluating the Thesis*

1. too specific, manageable, not that interesting.

EXERCISE 3-7 *For Practice: Writing the Outline*

Answers will vary.

Chapter 4

EXERCISE 4-1 *Topic Sentences*

1.   "I honestly believe that it [the Civil War] is in all our subconsciouses."

EXERCISE 4-2 *Organizing Paragraphs*

1. description

EXERCISE 4-3 *For Practice: Organizational Strategy*

Answers will vary.

EXERCISE 4-4 *Reiterating and Transitional Terms*

Answers will vary.

EXERCISE 4-5 *For Practice: Signaling Relationships with Transitional Terms*

Answers will vary

EXERCISE 4-6 *For Practice: Coherence*

Answers will vary.

EXERCISE 4-7 *Writing Effective Beginning and Ending Paragraphs*

Answers will vary.

Chapter 5

EXERCISE 5-1 *Responding to Drafts*

Answers will vary.

EXERCISE 5-2 *For Practice: Responding*

Answers will vary.

Chapter 6

EXERCISE 6-1 *Fallacies*

Answers will vary.

EXERCISE 6-2 *Critical Viewing*

Answers will vary

EXERCISE 6-3 *Visual Fallacies/Misleading Images*

Answers will vary.

EXERCISE 6-4 *For Practice*

Answers will vary.

Chapter 7

EXERCISE 7-1 *Develop and Organize a Rhetorical Analysis*
Answers will vary.

EXERCISE 7-2 *Analyze Images and Other Kinds of Visual Texts*
Answers will vary.

Chapter 8

EXERCISE 8-1 *Reflecting*
Answers will vary.

EXERCISE 8-2 *Identifying Focus*
Answers will vary.

EXERCISE 8-3 *Developing a Response*
Answers will vary.

EXERCISE 8-4 *For Practice*
Answers will vary.

Chapter 9

EXERCISE 9-1 *Finding an Informative Topic*
Answers will vary.

EXERCISE 9-2 *Sharpening Focus*
Answers will vary.

EXERCISE 9-3 *Organization*

1. chronological

EXERCISE 9-4 *Creating an Informative Essay*

Answers will vary.

EXERCISE 9-5 *For Practice*

Answers will vary.

Chapter 10

EXERCISE 10-1 *Arguable Claims*

1. statement of fact

EXERCISE 10-2 *Make an Arguable Claim*

Answers will vary.

EXERCISE 10-3 *Develop and Organize Good Reasons*

Answers will vary.

EXERCISE 10-4 *Argument*

Answers will vary.

EXERCISE 10-5 *A Persuasive Letter of Application and Résumé*

Answers will vary.

Chapter 11

EXERCISE 11-1 *Designing a Flyer*

Answers will vary.

Chapter 12

EXERCISE 12-1 *Deciding on Graphics*

1. pie chart
2. line graph

Chapter 13

EXERCISE 13-1 *For Practice: Oral Presentations*

Answers will vary.

EXERCISE 13-2 *Oral and Visual Presentations*

Answers will vary.

Chapter 14

EXERCISE 14-1 *Evaluating Web Sites*

Answers will vary.

EXERCISE 14-2 *For Practice: Audience and Purpose, Content, Readability, Visual Design, and Navigation*

Answers will vary.

Chapter 15

EXERCISE 15-1 *Research Strategy*

1. survey

EXERCISE 15-2 *Finding a Topic*

Answers will vary.

EXERCISE 15-3 *Developing A Working Thesis*

Answers will vary.

EXERCISE 15-4 *Primary and Secondary Research*

1. primary

Chapter 16

EXERCISE 16-1 *Libraries and/or Internet*

1. library

EXERCISE 16-2 *Identify Keywords*

Answers will vary.

EXERCISE 16-3 *Periodicals*

1. trade or scholarly

EXERCISE 16-4 *Creating a Bibliography*

Answers will vary.

Chapter 17

EXERCISE 17-1 *Find Articles and Other Sources in Library Databases*
Answers will vary.

EXERCISE 17-2 *Using Search Engines*
1. C, E

Chapter 18

EXERCISE 18-1 *Evaluating for Relevance and Reliability*
Answers will vary.

EXERCISE 18-2 *Relevance and Reliability*

Slightly relevant because it does not cover legislation. Very reliable, because it is a government site and has no commercial motive or bias. The information, however, is not current.

Chapter 19

EXERCISE 19-1 *Determining Plagiarism*
Example of scholastic dishonesty or plagiarism.

EXERCISE 19-2 *Using Citations*
No citation.

EXERCISE 19-3 *Using Quotes*
First sample sentence:

Tony Johnson, child survivor of abuse and AIDS and author of the best-selling book *A Rock and A Hard Place*, has a problem. Many of his celebrity friends don't believe he exists. One of the most outspoken of these friends is Armistead Maupin, who is, according to columnist Chris

Brice, "one of many thousands of people who have been moved by Tony Johnson's 1993 memoir."

EXERCISE 19-4 *Using Paraphrases*

1. correct

Chapter 20

EXERCISE 20-1 *Developing the Thesis*

Answers will vary.

EXERCISE 20-2 *Developing an Outline*

Answers will vary.

EXERCISE 20-3 *Using Quotes, Summaries, and Paraphrases*

1. quote

EXERCISE 20-4 *For Practice*

Answers will vary.

Chapter 21

EXERCISE 21-1 *Using MLA-style In-text Citation*

Answers will vary.

EXERCISE 21-2 *For Practice: MLA List of Works Cited*

Answers will vary.

EXERCISE 21-3 *MLA-style Comparison*

Answers will vary.

Chapter 22

EXERCISE 22-1 *Writing About Poetry*

Answers will vary.

EXERCISE 22-2 *Complex Arguments*

Answers will vary.

Chapter 23

EXERCISE 23-1 *APA References*

Answers will vary.

EXERCISE 23-2 *For Practice: Online Treasure Hunt for APA Cites*

Answers will vary.

Chapter 24

EXERCISE 24-1 *CMS References*

Answers will vary.

EXERCISE 24-2 *For Practice: Online Treasure Hunt for CMS Cites*

Answers will vary.

Chapter 25

EXERCISE 25-1 *CSE References*

Answers will vary.

Answers will vary.

Chapter 26

EXERCISE 26-1 *Active Voice*

Answers will vary. Here is sample sentence rewrite:

Researchers in neuroscience <u>have reported</u> that food advertising often <u>succeeds</u> because of the structure of our brains.

EXERCISE 26-2 *Strong Verbs*

Answers will vary. Here is a sample sentence rewrite:

Though few people celebrate the experience of pain, the human body **is** <u>dependent on unpleasant impulses</u> for survival.

EXERCISE 26-3 *Living Agents*

Answers will vary. Here is a sample sentence rewrite:

<u>The observation of these old customs</u> in parts of Europe where the inhabitants are Celtic proves their Druid origin.

Chapter 27

EXERCISE 27-1 *Rewriting the Wordy Passages*

Possible rewrite:

> Because we cannot see a black hole up-close, we must use our imaginations to consider its properties.

EXERCISE 27-2 *Empty Intensifiers*

Possible replacement:

> 1942, the American Office of Strategic Services (OSS) Chief William Donovan gathered six <u>incredibly respected</u> [prestigious] scientists to develop a truth serum.

EXERCISE 27-3 *Eliminate Wordiness*

Possible rewrite:

> The necktie is considered one of the oldest fashion creations and one of the earliest items created solely for decorating the human form.

EXERCISE 27-4 *Rewriting for Clarity and Concision*

Possible rewrite:

> There are a number of ways fossils can help paleontologists gain additional information about ancient eras.

Chapter 28

EXERCISE 28-1 *Combining Sentences for Emphasis*

Since popular representations of Jesus portrayed a thin, almost sickly man, men did not identify with Christianity as readily as women did.

EXERCISE 28-2 *Practice with Parallelism*

Sesame Street entered the American consciousness in 1969, playing, singing, and teaching.

EXERCISE 28-3 *Revising for Parallelism*

Answers will vary.

Chapter 29

EXERCISE 29-1 *Writing in Standard American English*

Possible revision:

> In her youth, Ride was a superb tennis player.

EXERCISE 29-2 *Formal or Informal?*

Possible rewrite:

Dear Ms. Le Chat,

I am writing to thank you again for arranging our delicious luncheon yesterday.

EXERCISE 29-3 *Eliminating Colloquial Language*

Possible rewrite:

The late David Brower was president of the Sierra Club, a group devoted to American wilderness preservation..

EXERCISE 29-4 *Connotations*

1. +   -   -   +   +   +   -   -   -
   thin, skinny, gaunt, slender, sleek, lean, emaciated, bony, skeletal,
   =   =
slight, lanky

EXERCISE 29-5 *Using Connotations*

Possible rewrite:

I'm not as happy with this paper as I have been with my previous ones for this class.

EXERCISE 29-6 *Using Specific Language*

Possible rewrite:

Space missions can adversely affect an astronaut's health.

EXERCISE 29-7 *Selecting the Right Word*

Butchering a hog requires (<u>patience</u>, patients) and hard work.

EXERCISE 29-8 *Figuring Out Figurative Phrasing*

Possible rewrite:

After the 1956 explosion, Bezymianny's ash blanketed the surrounding area; days later, the ash had traveled to Alaska and Britain.

EXERCISE 29-9 *Overusing Clichés*

Possible rewrite:

> However in Japan and in the Mediterranean, squid, octopus, and cuttlefish are an important food source and <u>sell like hotcakes</u> [sell well].

Chapter 30

EXERCISE 30-1 *Eliminating Stereotypes*

Possible rewrite:

> Throughout the New York City boroughs, widely diverse groups live and work together.

EXERCISE 30-2 *Using Inclusive Language: Gender and Sexual Orientation*

Possible rewrite:

> Following his campaign promise, President Clinton pursued the annihilation of the military policy that limited the enlistment based on sexual orientation.

EXERCISE 30-3 *Using Inclusive Language: Race/Ethnicity*

By identifying where <u>old people</u> [people over the age of sixty-five] live, for example, questions regarding politics, special interests, and marketing can be answered.

Chapter 31

EXERCISE 31-1 *Understand English as a Global Language*

Answers will vary.

EXERCISE 31-2 *Respect Differences in Language and Culture*

Answers will vary.

Chapter 32

EXERCISE 32-1 *Sentence Patterns*

1. imperative, negative, active

EXERCISE 32-2 *Functions of Nouns*

The boyish <u>Ronald Reagan</u> [subject] was the studio's first <u>choice</u> [subject complement] for the male <u>lead</u> [object of preposition].

EXERCISE 32-3 *Functions of Pronouns*

The ramming was no accident; after the whale hit the *Essex* once, <u>it</u> [personal pronoun] turned around to hit the ship a second time.

EXERCISE 32-4 *Functions of Verbs*

Frank Oz <u>was</u> [aux modal] <u>born</u> [main] in Hereford, England, in 1944 and <u>began</u> [aux modal] <u>staging</u> [main] puppet shows when he was 12.

EXERCISE 32-5 *Verbals*

The evil eye is a <u>focused</u> [past participle] gaze, supposedly <u>causing</u> [present participle] death and destruction.

EXERCISE 32-6 *Modifiers*

Parker's father encouraged her to pursue "<u>feminine</u> arts" [adjective modifying *arts*] such as piano and poetry, but <u>just</u> following his death in 1913, she rushed into what turned out to be a <u>profitable</u> foray into the world of literature.

EXERCISE 32-7 *Prepositional Phrases*

Johnson's campaign, inspired by the New Deal of Franklin Roosevelt's administration, was attractive to members of both political parties.

EXERCISE 32-8 *Subordinate and Coordinate Conjunctions*

Only four of the 400 species of shark attack humans: bull sharks, whitetips, tiger sharks, <u>and</u> great whites.

EXERCISE 32-9 *Identifying Word Classes*

On a [article] clear Texas [noun] morning in February of 2003, onlookers waited patiently [adverb] to observe the reentry and landing of the space shuttle *Columbia*.

EXERCISE 32-10 *Clause Patterns*

1. *subject–verb–object*

EXERCISE 32-11 *Kinds of Clauses*

1. Tribes in the West Indies who sought dominance over neighboring peoples [adjective clause] often ate human flesh.

EXERCISE 32-12 *Identify the Phrases*

1. Arriving on Ellis Island, [participle phrase] immigrants seeking American citizenship [participle phrase] were herded into long lines [prepositional phrase] for medical inspection. [prepositional phrase]

EXERCISE 32-13 *Clauses*

2. The dead reappear during the month-long celebration. [simple]

EXERCISE 32-14 *Complex Sentences*

Possible Solution:

1. **Compound**:

   Philip K. Wrigley was a chewing gum entrepreneur, but he also began the All-American Girls Professional Baseball League in 1943.

   Complex:

   In 1943, when the onset of World War II threatened American interest in the sport of baseball, Philip K. Wrigley, chewing gum entrepreneur, began the All-American Girls Professional Baseball League.

   Compound-Complex:

   Philip K. Wrigley was primarily known as a chewing gum entrepreneur, but in 1943, when the onset of American involvement in

World War II threatened interest in baseball, he pioneered the All-American Girls Professional Baseball League.

Chapter 33

EXERCISE 33-1 *Sentence Fragments*

1. Flying squirrels are like typical squirrels except they have flaps of skin that allow them to glide.

EXERCISE 33-2 *Revising to Eliminate Fragments*

Possible rewrite:

Barton Springs still seems like a place not in Texas for those who come from elsewhere, with its surrounding hills covered by live oaks and mountain juniper, and the ground around the pool shaded by pecan trees whose trunks are a dozen feet in circumference.

EXERCISE 33-3 *Run-on Sentences*

1. The original Kabuki troupes were mostly comprised of female dancers; however, male performers replaced them after the art became associated with prostitution.

EXERCISE 33-4 *Comma Splices*

1. Riefenstahl spent her early days performing in Germany as a dancer. However, a 1924 knee injury derailed her dance career, detouring her into a successful, scandal-ridden life in film.

Chapter 34

EXERCISE 34-1 *Verb Tense Review*

1. Aaron plays the piano.

EXERCISE 34-2 *Singular and Plural Subjects*

2. Each Italian city and town in Italy possesses a historical rationale for the gastronomical traditions of today.

EXERCISE 34-3 *"One of Those" Exercises*

1. Born in south Texas in 1911 and overcome with a passion for sports, Didrikson ☐aharias was not one of those girls who were wiling away the hours dreaming of wearing dresses, catching boys, and settling down.

EXERCISE 34-4 *Indefinite Pronouns*

1. Of those who overcame the gender barrier, few are more beloved than Lily Tomlin, the creator of Ernestine, the telephone operator, and Edith Ann, the precocious child in the jumbo rocking chair.

EXERCISE 34-5 *Collective Nouns*

The administration usually [try/tries] to avoid responsibility for issues concerning students living off campus, but also [listen/listens]…

EXERCISE 34-6 *Tricky Subjects*

1. African-American theatrics [singular] dates back to 1821, the year John Brown organized the first troupe of African-American actors.

Chapter 35

EXERCISE 35-1 *Verb Forms*

Recent lobbying [present participle-gerund] efforts by animal rights groups are illustrating [present participle-present perfect] how drastically contemporary beliefs regarding [present participle-gerund] animal safety differ [base form] from beliefs in medieval times.

EXERCISE 35-2 *Irregular Verbs*

After marrying in 1940, Lucille Ball and Desi Arnaz [strived/strove] to create their own television situation comedy.

EXERCISE 35-3 *Transitive and Intransitive Verbs*

1. A rattlesnake will often [lay/<u>lie</u>] in wait for its favorite meal: a rat.

EXERCISE 35-4 *Verb Tense Review*

Native American activists, including Dennis Banks and Russell Means, [<u>created</u>/ create] AIM, a militant organization to fight for civil rights for American Indians.

EXERCISE 35-5 *Indicating Mood*

Using the slogan "Let's <u>get</u> [imperative] this country moving again..."

EXERCISE 35-6 *Subjunctive Forms*

Rapture of the deep results when nitrogen levels elevate in the bloodstream because of added pressure, and the diver begins to feel as if she [was/<u>were</u>] invincible.

Chapter 36

EXERCISE 36-1 *Picky about Pronouns*

If <u>you</u> and a friend go on a road trip, the ADA suggests that <u>you</u> and ~~her~~ she limit <u>your</u> stops at fast food restaurants.

EXERCISE 36-2 *Whose Pronoun is it Anyway?*

Seats in Japanese Parliament have lately gone to candidates who have high ambitions, fame, and no political experience.

EXERCISE 36-3 *Pronoun Review*

1. The gurkhas are a division in the British armed forces (<u>who</u>/whom) originate from Nepal.

EXERCISE 36-4 *Determining the Antecedent*

1. Canine experts disagree on the origin of the <u>name</u> "Greyhound", but may believe it derives from "Greek Hound."

EXERCISE 36-5 *Pronoun Review II*

Neither the three <u>films</u> nor the stage <u>play</u> used (their) **its** time to tell the complete and accurate story of the real Maria von Trapp...

EXERCISE 36-6 *Pronouns and Gender Bias*

1. When people become financially overextended, they often consider credit cards as a way of making ends meet.

Chapter 37

EXERCISE 37-1 *Comparatives and Superlatives*

1. The best selling car in the United States is the Toyota Camry, closely followed by the Honda Accord and the Ford Taurus.

EXERCISE 37-2 *Double Negatives*

After the creation of the House Un-American Activities Committee (HUAC), Cold War paranoia could barely hide itself in post-World War II America.

EXERCISE 37-3 *Tricky Adjective / Adverb Pairs*

In the early days of manned space missions, NASA had [<u>fewer</u>/less] problems feeding astronauts.

EXERCISE 37-4 *Ambiguous Phrases and Clauses*

1. <u>Now known as Juneteenth</u>, Texas celebrates the day Texan slaves discovered their freedom.

Rewrite: Now known as Juneteenth, the day Texans slaves discovered their freedom is celebrated in Texas.

EXERCISE 37-5 *Ambiguous Adjectives*

Lynn rose from a <u>Kentucky sheltered</u> [sheltered Kentucky] childhood to earn the title "First Lady of Country Music," garnering awards <u>various</u> [various awards] and honors.

EXERCISE 37-6 *Squinting Modifiers*

Mendel's work <u>initially</u> focused on hybridizing the Lathyrus, or sweet pea.

EXERCISE 37-7 *Descriptive Modifiers*

In the thirteenth and fourteenth centuries, the Italian Papal States, <u>because of militantly rivaling families</u>, were consumed in chaos. [In the thirteenth and fourteenth centuries, the Italian Papal States were consumed in chaos because of militantly rivaling families.]

EXERCISE 37-8 *Dangling Modifiers*

2. Lasting for three days in June of 1967, Monterey presented over thirty artists.

Chapter 38

EXERCISE 38-1 *Comma Review*

1. King cobras, in fact, have a poisonous bite from the moment they are born.

EXERCISE 38-2 *Commas and Coordinating Conjunctions*

1. The band Abba was only together from 1974 to 1982[,] yet their hit "Dancing Queen" is still popular today.

EXERCISE 38-3 *Modifiers and Commas*

Trajan decided to use the Empire's coffers, <u>which were brimming with war booty</u>, to begin a massive building program. (nonrestrictive modifier)

EXERCISE 38-4 *Series and Commas*

2. White-tailed deer and coyotes are among the animals that have adapted best to urban habitats.

EXERCISE 38-5 *Adjective Series and Commas*

While an <u>average, meat-eating</u> [coordinate] American eats approximately 70 pounds of pork per year, China leads the world in pork consumption.

EXERCISE 38-6 *Comma Review*

Craquelure is "the fine network of cracks that scores the surface of paintings."

EXERCISE 38-7 *More on Commas*

Cario[,] Egypt

EXERCISE 38-8 *Clarifying with Commas*

Because geologists used both radiometric and fossil dating[,] we now know that the Colorado River only started carving the Grand Canyon five or six million years ago.

Chapter 39

EXERCISE 39-1 *Semicolon Review*

The media reported that the wreckage of a flying saucer was discovered on a ranch near Roswell; however, military spokespeople came up with another explanation.

EXERCISE 39-2 *Colon Review*

The House on Mango Street tells the story of a Mexican American girl who has a telling name: Esperanza (Hope).

Chapter 40

EXERCISE 40-1 *Hyphen Review*

Independent candidates are often viewed as fly-by-night long shots with little or no hope of winning positions of power.

Chapter 41

EXERCISE 41-1 *Using Punctuation for Emphasis*

Coffea arabica (the official name for the bean) was made popular in Yemen.

EXERCISE 41-2 *Setting off Information*

1. Naples is a dirty and noisy metropolis in a spectacular setting–a city that sprawls around the Bay of Naples with Mount Vesuvius at its back, facing out to the islands of Procida, Ischia, and Capri.

EXERCISE 41-3 *Parentheses Review*

To get on the show, an artist had to have: (1) style, (2) twang, and (3) the Nashville sound.

Chapter 42

EXERCISE 42-1 *Missing Apostrophes*

Survivors' stories contain accounts of tunneling through up to sixteen feet of debris after the disaster.

EXERCISE 42-2 *Missing Apostrophes*

Texas VIPs and international diplomats alike affectionately referred to Lyndon B. Johnson as Big Daddy.

Chapter 43

EXERCISE 43-1 *Quotations and Punctuation*

Horowitz's difficulty was finding words that might, "make sense to anyone but a fellow addict."

EXERCISE 43-2 *Other Uses for Quotation Marks*

Humans have been divided into several primary races according to physical traits.

EXERCISE 43-3 *Punctuation and Quotations*

What does Allison mean when she tells gay and lesbian writers, "We must aim much higher than just staying alive if we are to begin to approach our true potential"?

Chapter 44

EXERCISE 44-1 *Periods*

Ms. Friedan was born Feb. 4, 1921.

EXERCISE 44-2 *Missing Punctuation*

Betty Friedan's *The Feminine Mystique* addressed the question, "Is this all?"

EXERCISE 44-3 *Punctuation and Elliptical Phrasing*

Ward notes, "The phenomenon of the waning star is heavily represented in the last century of English and American culture. . . "

EXERCISE 44-4 *Punctuation Review*

In 1996 alone, over sixty deaths occurred due to religious snake handling.

Chapter 45

EXERCISE 45-1 *Spelling*

Tutu maintains that this is true for whites as well as blacks, a position that isn't popular with some South Africans.

EXERCISE 45-2 *Homophones*

Modern day Cambodia, or Kampuchea, gained its independence from France in 1953, but (by/buy) the early 1970s the country was embroiled in bloody civil war.

EXERCISE 45-3 *Adding Suffixes*

1. slapped

Exercise 45-4 *Adding Suffixes to Silent E's*

1. definitely

EXERCISE 45-5 *Plurals*

Wilde, a successful author with two children and multiple followers in literary London, made a mistake when he pressed charges against the famous lord.

EXERCISE 45-6 *Spelling Rules*

There are several kinds of sleep disorders, the most common being insomnia.

Chapter 47

EXERCISE 46-1 *Capitalization Review*

The Federal Bureau of Investigation (FBI) has long been considered an American institution that was fathered by President Theodore Roosevelt.

EXERCISE 46-2 *When to Italicize*

Films such as Tonight or Never preserve Chanel's designs for future generations, while the failed Broadway musical Coco attempts to embody her life's work.

EXERCISE 47-1 *Deciding When to Abbreviate*

Though it erupted in 79AD, Mount Vesuvius is still famous because of its violent decimation of the city of Pompeii.

EXERCISE 47-2 *Using Acronyms Correctly*

Various organizations define torture in different ways; however, United Nations Declaration Against Torture (UNDAT) officially defines torture as undue pain suffered at the hands of a public official.

EXERCISE 47-3 *Word-Numbers or Numerals*

She may be one of over 9.5 million people suffering from TMJ, a condition that often causes symptoms such as popping, swelling, and aching in the jaw.

Chapter 48

EXERCISE 48-1 *Understand How Languages Differ*

Answers will vary.

Chapter 49

EXERCISE 49-1 *Common Nouns*

In 1903, Chicago opened the new Iroquois Theater on West Randolph Street.

EXERCISE 49-2 *Plural Nouns*

1. In the late 1950s, Detroit was one of America's [many city, cities)] famous for the production of [numbers of automobile, automobiles].

EXERCISE 49-3 *Singular/Plural Inconsistencies*

Every year, thousands of brides and grooms don traditional attire while attending their weddings; one garment associated with many of these traditional weddings is the groom's cummerbund or decorative waistband.

EXERCISE 49-4 *Choosing the Right Article*

In [a/an/the] early 1900s, boxing films were [a/an/the] extremely popular form of entertainment; [a/an/the] fight would be filmed and shown in movie houses across [a/an/the] country.

EXERCISE 49-5 *Article Review*

While Americans recovered from a [the] Vietnam War [singular count)] Gary Dahl sat in the [a] California restaurant [singular count] talking with friends.

Chapter 50

EXERCISE 50-1 *To Be or Not To Be*

Though many think it simply marks the Jewish New Year, Rosh Hashanah actually [was conceiving/ was conceived] with a four-fold meaning.

EXERCISE 50-2 *Modal Auxiliary Verbs*

1. In the 1970s, the Kerr-McGee plutonium plant was accused of violations that may [possibility] shall have endangered worker's lives.

EXERCISE 50-3 *Missing Parts of Sentences*

1. The evil Koshchei the Deathless would attempt [you to hide/to hide)] under a giant oak tree.

EXERCISE 50-4 *Verbs + Gerunds or Infinitives*

1. Historians risk [misidentifying/to misidentify] actual origins when stories have been passed down simply by word of mouth.

EXERCISE 50-5 *Conditional Categories*

1.   If a fraternity boy wants to become engaged to his girlfriend, he pins his fraternity pin on her blouse.

EXERCISE 50-6 *Participle Adjectives*

Many <u>tornadoes</u> are <u>created</u> by a special   <u>rotating</u> <u>thunderstorm</u> called a <u>supercell</u>.

Chapter 51

EXERCISE 51-1 *Subjects in Sentences*

Though some <u>assassins</u> are widely known, <u>Charles Guiteau</u> and   <u>Leon Czolgolsz</u> are relatively obscure.

EXERCISE 51-2 *Independent Clauses*

1.   Geologists based the theory on an earlier one that <u>had observed that the continents fit together like pieces of a puzzle</u>.

EXERCISE 51-3 *Labeling Parts of Sentences*

1.   Ganesh (S) is (LV) the god (SC) of good luck (PP).

EXERCISE 51-4 *Confusing Modifiers*

1.   Kurosawa chose <u>initially</u> painting as his preferred career. (Adverb between verb and direct object)

EXERCISE 51-5 *Correct Placement of Adjectives and Adverbs*

1.   By the <u>fourteenth</u> century, <u>early</u> cards   <u>playing</u> were used   <u>widely</u> (frequency) for gambling and predicting the future.

EXERCISE 51-6 *Dangling Modifiers*

1.   Robespierre followed the writings of Jean Jacques Rousseau, his philosophical role model.

Chapter 52

EXERCISE 52-1 *Preposition Review*

[In, On, <u>At</u>] this time, pilots were familiar [<u>with,</u> in, on] the "Wall of Air" that existed [in, on, <u>at</u>] the speed of sound.

EXERCISE 52-2 *Adjective-preposition Phrases*

The United States remains [<u>grateful to</u>/grateful with] the people of France for the gift of the Statue of Liberty.